D0340687

I Was Right on Time

Buck O'Neil
with Steve Wulf and David Conrads

Simon & Schuster

SIMON & SCHUSTER
Rockefeller Center
1230 Avenue of the Americas
New York, NY 10020

SIMON & SCHUSTER and colophon are registered trademarks
of Simon & Schuster Inc.

A leatherbound signed first edition of this book has been
published by Easton Press.

Designed by Levavi & Levavi

Manufactured in the United States of America

10 9 8 7 6 5 4 3 2 1

Library of Congress Cataloging-in-Publication Data

O'Neil, Buck, date
   I was right on time / Buck O'Neil with Steve Wulf
and David Conrads.
      p.   cm.
   Includes index.
   1. O'Neil, Buck, 1911-   . 2. Baseball play-
ers—United States—Biography. 3. Afro-American
baseball players—Biography. 4. Negro leagues—
History. 5. 796.357/092 B. I. Wulf, Steve.
II. Conrads, David. III. Title.
GV865.O48A3   1996   96-6370   CIP
ISBN 0-684-80305-4

All photographs appear courtesy of Buck O'Neil,
except where otherwise indicated.

Acknowledgments

With deepest appreciation I acknowledge the encouragement and assistance of those persons who made valuable contributions in the making of this book. I'd like to thank the members of the Society for American Baseball Research (SABR) for all their help; Ken Burns for including me in his celebrated *Baseball* documentary; and writer Mark Ribowsky for his editorial assistance. Most importantly, I extend a special thank-you to all the men of the Negro leagues who fill my life with competitive spirits. They live in my memory as much as in this book.

And finally, I want to thank my friends and colleagues who encouraged me to write about my baseball travels. Their persistence was motivation for me to remember events that my memory had denied me. It was truly a glorious time, and I am so glad to have been a part of it.

John "Buck" O'Neil

To my beloved wife of fifty years, Ora Lee Owen-O'Neil, for her enduring patience during my playing days. She stood by me and ran our household while I was traveling with the Monarchs and later scouting for the Cubs. Her sacrifices allowed me to play with some of the best players in the world. I will always be thankful for the presence of this cheerful and easy-to-love lady.

Contents

Foreword

We live in an age of celebrities, not heroes. Even the word "hero" seems to be something out of the past, out of a time when great men were still possible, an age of unambiguous deeds and values worthy of sacrifice. In studying the history of baseball, our national game that mirrors so much of our history and so many of its faults and virtues, I learned a great deal about the sport's hidden history, the darker side that is in so many ways more revealing than the sanitized version we are spoon-fed by our media. I am convinced that this hidden history is the key to our salvation; by lifting up the rug of our past, we find not only the sins we hoped we had concealed beneath it, but also new and powerful heroes who thrived in the darkness and can teach us much about how to live in the light.

John Jordan O'Neil is a hero, not in the superficial sporting sense of a man who homers in the ninth to win a game, but in the human sense of a man we all should look to and strive to be more like. His life reflects the past and contains many of the bitter experiences that our country reserved to men of his color, but there is no bitterness in him; it's not so much that he put that suffering behind him as that he has brought gold and light out of bitterness and despair, loneliness and suffering. He knows that he can go farther with generosity and kindness than with anger and hate. He is wise, funny, self-deprecating, and absolutely sure of what he wants from life. He is my hero, my friend, my mentor; he is, like Abraham Lincoln and Jackie Robinson, what human progress is all about.

From the moment I first saw Buck O'Neil, in interviews conducted by my partner Lynn Novick for our *Baseball* series, I sensed an electricity about him that made him unlike anyone I've ever met. Since that first glimpse, Buck and I have become not just friends, but as close as friends can be—and really more like family than just friends. (I can still see the face of the ticket agent at the Delta Air Lines counter when I asked for a family rate on the Boston–New York shuttle for the four of us—Buck, me, my then seven-year-old daughter, Lilly, and my eleven-year-old daughter, Sarah—and the sight of Lilly and Buck hugging that convinced the agent that "family" was the word that best described us.) I've heard him speak to groups a hundred times—he's heard me as often—and at the end of every talk he leaves each listener convinced he is the one person Buck got up that morning to speak to, the one person Buck has been waiting to see. There's nothing you can say about Buck O'Neil that one second in his presence won't prove a hundred times over. It is impossible to resist the positive force that lights him from within and then spreads out and lights and warms you, too. No one is immune to him; only the inattentive miss what is special about him.

One time, early in the interviewing process for *Baseball*, we brought Buck up to lily-white Walpole, New Hampshire—lily-white in every sense, from the population to the snow-covered Currier & Ives setting—where we filmed some more interviews and he got to meet some of our editing staff. We all went out to lunch at a little pizza place; it was the first time the staff, who'd seen him on film, had spent any time with him in person. (I always envy people who are meeting Buck for the first time; whether they meet him in a bar or are sitting next to him on a plane, they may not know who this elegant older gentleman is at first, but by the end of their passage they're converts.) A woman who's been with me from the beginning of my work, Susanna, went up to Buck at the start of the lunch and said to him, very formally, "Mr. O'Neil, it's a pleasure to meet you," shook his hand and went back to where she was sitting. So we all had our pizza, and we talked, and then at the end of the meal Susanna went over to Buck again, stuck out her hand, and said, "Mr. O'Neil, it's truly been a pleasure." Well, Buck didn't move, just looked at her, and there was a mortifying pause as her hand stood there in midair, with Buck making no move to take it in his. And then, slowly, gracefully, he stood up, smiled, and opened his arms to her and said, "Give it up." And she just flew into his arms. "Give it up"—that's Buck's way. "Give me a hug," yes, but also, don't be so formal, don't hide behind polite conventions, don't be afraid to show someone some love. Show what's in your heart, always; don't keep it inside. Give it up.

July 28, 1995 was Buck O'Neil Day in Kansas City; there was a ceremony at Kaufman Stadium, and a lot of the old Monarchs came to attend the game. The next day, my birthday, Buck and I flew together to Chicago before splitting off in different directions—I was going home, and he was going to Cooperstown for the long-awaited induction of his late friend Leon Day into the Baseball Hall of Fame. As we were parting at

O'Hare Airport, he turned to me and said, "You know, I've been talking to people and saying these same things for sixty years now, but now people are *hearing* me." There are no words, no prize, no tribute to anything I will ever do, no birthday present, that could mean more to me than that simple sentence from this remarkable man. And there was only one thing I could do: I had to give it up.

In these pages you will meet the Buck O'Neil I love, and you will learn about his life—and probably about your own as well. Listen, and hear, and cherish the wisdom of this holy man who is a gift to us all.

—Ken Burns, 1996

I Was Right
on Time

Chapter 1

Why, Nancy, There You Are

Call me Buck.

I was born John Jordan O'Neil, Junior, on November 13, 1911, in Carrabelle, Florida, and a few close friends still call me John, including my best friend, Ora Lee Owens, the beautiful woman I married fifty years ago. I have been called Jay, Foots, Country, and Cap, and also Nancy, which is a story I'll get to involving my friend Leroy "Satchel" Paige. I have been called a few names that shouldn't be spoken, and one time I was called something that made me laugh out loud. A few years ago, they were having a big eightieth birthday celebration for me at my African Methodist Episcopal Church in Kansas City, Missouri. There was all this babbling about Buck O'Neil did *this* and Buck O'Neil did *that.* But just in case any of it went to my head, a young boy I knew came up to me afterwards and introduced his friend to me; he said, "I'd like you to meet Buck O'Neil. He's an *old relic* from the Negro leagues." I said, "Son, you are *so* right."

I might have stayed an old relic, too, had it not been for another friend, Mr. Ken Burns. Ken was nice enough to keep his camera on me for a long time when he was making his documentary, *Baseball,* and thanks to that film, a whole new generation of people call me Buck. It's kind of nice to be discovered when you're eighty-two years old.

The best thing about the film, though, was that it gave me a chance to tell folks about the Negro leagues, about what a glorious enterprise black baseball was, and about what a wonderful thing *baseball* is. Back in 1981, at a reunion of us Negro league players in Ashland, Kentucky, a young fellow from *Sports Illustrated* asked me if I had any regrets, coming along as I did before Jackie Robinson integrated the major leagues. And this is what I told him then, and what I'm telling you now:

There is nothing greater for a human being than to get his body to react to all the things one does on a ballfield. It's as good as sex; it's as good as music. It fills you up. Waste no tears for me. I didn't come along too early—I was right on time.

You see, I don't have a bitter story. I truly believe I have been blessed. Growing up as I did in Sarasota, Florida, I saw men like John McGraw and Babe Ruth and Connie Mack during spring training. As a first baseman for the great Kansas City Monarchs, I played with and against men like Satchel Paige and Josh Gibson and Cool Papa Bell. As the manager of the Monarchs and later as a scout and a coach—the first African-American coach in the majors—for the Chicago Cubs, I got to see the young Ernie Banks, the young Lou Brock, the young Bo Jackson.

The first time I saw Ruth, up in St. Petersburg, it wasn't so much the *sight* of him that got to me as the *sound.* When Ruth was hitting the ball, it was a distinct sound, like a small stick of dynamite going off. You could tell it was Ruth and not Gehrig and not Lazzeri. The next time I heard that sound was in 1938, my first year with the Monarchs. We were in Griffith Stadium in Washington to play the Homestead Grays, and I heard that sound all the way up in the clubhouse, so I ran down to the dugout in just my pants and my sweatshirt to see who was hitting the ball. And it was Josh Gibson. I thought, my land, that's a powerful man.

I didn't hear it again for almost fifty years. I thought I'd never hear it again. But I was at Royals Stadium, scouting the American League for the Cubs, and I came out of the press room and was going down to field level when I heard that ball sound as if the Babe or Josh were still down there. *Pow! Pow! Pow!* It was Bo Jackson—the Royals had just called him up. And I'll tell you this: I'm going to keep going to the ballpark until I hear that sound again.

I have another reason for sticking around: Sometimes I think the Lord has kept me on this earth as long as He has so I can bear witness to the Negro leagues. I'm fortunate enough to be a member of the Veterans Committee for the Baseball Hall of Fame. Monte Irvin and I are the only Negro league players on the committee now that Roy Campanella has passed on, and for years I've been putting forward the names of the players I think belong in the Hall.

Oh, we've been represented very well in Cooperstown ever since 1971, when Satchel Paige became the first black man to be named to the Hall based on his Negro league career alone. Josh Gibson and my namesake, the great Buck Leonard, who played first base like I did and was our answer to Lou Gehrig, went in the next year, followed by Monte Irvin, Cool Papa Bell, Judy Johnson, and Oscar Charleston.

These men were elected by a special committee set

up by Commissioner Bowie Kuhn specifically to nominate Negro league ballplayers. When the committee was done with its work in 1977, it fell to the Veterans Committee to make the nominations, and over the next four years John Henry Lloyd, the great Cuban Martin Dihigo, and Rube Foster, the father of the Negro leagues, got in. But then things slowed down. It took until 1987 before Ray Dandridge made it in, and then nothing happened for eight more years.

The problem was, the Veterans Committee votes on all kinds of managers, umpires, baseball executives, and the ballplayers who were passed over by the baseball writers when they were eligible for admission. The committee could elect only up to two people each year, and, being one of the eighteen people on the committee, I could see how tough it was for any of the Negro league players to get the 75 percent of the vote they needed. Listen, it's hard enough to get fourteen people to agree on anything.

But the Negro league ballplayers were at a greater disadvantage because the other candidates were getting a second crack, while the Negro leaguers had never been voted on at all by the writers, because Negro league players aren't on the original ballot. They don't get all the publicity that other players get for making it or just missing when the writers' votes are announced every year. So I got to thinking, and

I talked to the committee and the Hall of Fame people about it, and we were able to change the rules to make it a little easier for the Negro league players.

It sounds strange, but I told them, "You got to start putting us in a separate category the way you did fifty years ago." They call that ironical, but all I know is that it worked out. There are about a dozen men left who deserve their own plaques, but the one guy I was concentrating on was Leon Day, a great little pitcher *and* a fast little outfielder for the Newark Eagles, among other teams. The reason I wanted Leon in was that he was still alive, living down in Baltimore in ill health.

So, last March, when the Veterans Committee elected Richie Ashburn and William Hulbert, we also elected Leon Day. Leon was in the hospital when he got the word, and a week later he passed away, knowing he was a Hall of Famer. We made it just in time with Leon.

The problem is, the Hall only gave us five years to rectify this unfair situation, which isn't enough time, because we've got more than four players who should be in the Hall of Fame. Just off the top of my head, I can rattle off about a dozen, pitchers like Bullet Joe Rogan and Smokey Joe Williams and Willie Foster and Hilton Smith and Cannonball Redding. Hitters like Turkey Stearnes and Mule Suttles and Louis Santop and Biz Mackey and Willard Brown and Ted Strong, and slick fielders like Willie Wells. There are 82 players from the major leagues during the years the Negro leagues existed who are in the Hall; it stands to reason that more than eleven of us were good enough to be worthy of the honor, too.

Some folks are saying maybe I belong in that Hall, too. But I'm honest with myself about it. If people say it, it's probably because of the Ken Burns series, not because they saw me play ball. The truth is, I don't belong; I was a very good ballplayer, but very good ballplayers don't belong in the Hall of Fame. Great ballplayers do. Oh, I'd like to think I might get in the Hall one day, but maybe as a manager or for other contributions that I made to baseball. Right now, my job is seeing to it that the guys I know are qualified to get in *do* get in.

Looking around now, there are getting to be fewer and fewer of us old Negro-leaguers. But whenever we get together nowadays, we have a fine time recalling our playing days. It's interesting how much we've improved over the years. We started out as good players, but as the years go by, we just get better and better. Why, it's amazing how great we were! We could do things the players of today can only dream of. That's not true, of course, but the way we talk, you'd think it was.

But the sad thing is that, like with Leon Day, when we do get together it's usually at funerals. And with every Negro league player we bury, we say goodbye to another person who can testify to the glory of *our* times. We might not have played in the major leagues, but we kept the faith and cleared the path for Jackie Robinson. We might not have batted against Lefty Grove or pitched to Ted Williams, but we had to stand in against Bullet Joe Rogan and face Josh Gibson. It's like I said at Satchel's funeral in 1982: People say it's a shame he never pitched against the best. But who's to say he didn't?

A lot of people think that Negro baseball was like that movie with James Earl Jones, Richard Pryor, and Billy Dee Williams, *The Bingo Long Traveling All-Stars & Motor Kings.* But we were no minstrel show. We didn't just all pile into a Cadillac and pick up a game here and there—although there were times when I did some of that stuff. I had to if I wanted to keep eating. That was reality. But in the Negro leagues proper, we had a schedule and we had coverage by newspapers and we had league commissioners and league presidents. Like the white big-league fellows, we had spring training down South. We had an all-star game every year for over twenty years in Comiskey Park, and we outdrew the white all-star game some of those years, when we'd have fifty thousand people looking at us. Most years, we had a World Series, too.

Mostly, though, we had a *tradition* of professional men, going back to the 1800s when Moses Fleetwood Walker was the first black man to play in the big leagues around 1884 before they hounded him out of the game. Black baseball wasn't organized until 1920, but black men had been playing since the Civil War, and there were great players and great teams the whole time, teams like the Philadelphia Giants and the Cuban Giants—who were really black—and the Indianapolis ABCs and the Algona Brownies and the Tennessee Rats. Then came the Chicago American Giants and Kansas City Monarchs and Homestead Grays and Pittsburgh Crawfords and Newark Eagles.

At one time, we had three or four leagues playing all at once, the Negro National League, Negro American League, Negro Southern League, Negro Western League, and so on. We had black and white businessmen, brilliant men like J. L. Wilkinson, a wonderful and kind man who owned my Kansas City Monarchs. Show you how smart Wilkie was, he invented night baseball five years before the big leagues got around to playing at night, though when they did nobody ever gave him any credit.

And we had names. We had Fox and Piggy and Bunny and Possum and Groundhog and Rats and

Mule and Frog and Burro and Early-bird and Goose and Turkey. Turkey, whose name you've already come across, was really Norman Stearnes, one of the greatest hitters and strangest men I have ever had the pleasure of knowing. They called him Turkey because of the way he flapped his arms around when he ran. You expected Turkey to take off and fly when he was running, but I was more fascinated by his devotion to hitting. Turkey carried around his bats, a thirty-four-incher and a thirty-five-incher, in a special bat case, like they were violins. One time, after a tough loss, the Monarchs were in the hotel eating dinner, and the manager, Frank Duncan, asked me to go check on the Gobbler—that's another thing we called Turkey, you see. So I knocked on the Gobbler's door, and he said, "Come in," and there he was, sitting in the middle of his bed dressed in his pajamas talking to his bats. He said to the 34-incher, "I used you and only hit the ball up against the fence." Then he turned to the 35-incher and said, "If I had picked you, I would have hit the ball over the fence and we would have tied the game." Strange man, but Turkey's another guy who belongs in the Hall of Fame.

Man, did we have names. We had Sea Boy and Gunboat, Steel Arm and Copperknee, Darknight and Skin Down, Mosquito and Jitterbug, Popsickle and Popeye, Suitcase and, of course, Satchel. Our trainer with the

Monarchs was Jewbaby Floyd—I can't recollect why we called him that, and I can't remember what his real first name was. There were some pitchers with great nicknames, Steel Arm Davis, Ankleball Moss—that's where that mean sonuvagun threw the ball from, his ankles—and Cocaina Garcia. Cocaina, whom I used to face down in Cuba, got his name from his wicked curveball, which made all us hitters go numb.

As for my own names, well, there are some pretty simple explanations for them—and some pretty complicated ones, too. Jay, or J.J., is what the members of my family called me when I was growing up in Carrabelle and Sarasota. "Jay," my father would tell me, "when I'm away, you're the man of the house." Along with the responsibility, my father passed on some of his baseball talent. When I was fourteen, the local semipro team, the Sarasota Tigers, asked my school principal Emma Booker if they could borrow me to play first base. By then, I had a nickname as well as a position: Foots. That's because I had pretty big dogs, size eleven since I was twelve.

It was Ox Clemons, the great coach at Edward Waters College in Jacksonville, who gave me my next handle. I had gone to Edward Waters straight out of eighth grade because they didn't allow blacks at Sarasota High School—only four high schools in the whole state did. (I finally did get my diploma from

Sarasota High in the spring of 1995—sixty-four years after my original class graduated!) Ox saw my rural ways pretty quickly among his city boys, and he started calling me Country. Cap, short for Captain, was a name that came along later in life, when I was manager of the Monarchs, and it's what one of my first base coaches, Mr. Lionel Hampton—the same Lionel Hampton who's a magician on the vibes, even in his eighties—calls me to this day.

But it was Buck that stuck, which is funny because that one was purely a case of mistaken identity. I left Edward Waters in 1934 to go play for the Miami Giants, a pretty good team that was owned by a man named Buck O'Neal—that's right, a different spelling. Although I'm not proud of it, a few years later I was playing in a grass skirt for the barnstorming Zulu Cannibal Giants, a team that was owned by Abe Saperstein, a big-time promoter of Negro league games in the Midwest who also started the Harlem Globetrotters. Abe was perfecting the Globetrotters' act with us ballplayers, even though we hated doing things like wearing the grass skirt, putting war paint on our faces, and generally acting like a bunch of fools to draw white folks to the park—though, let me say, I don't believe many white fans came just to see us clown around. Most had respect for us as ballplayers and would've come regardless.

Anyway, the promoter of the Zulu Cannibal Giants was Syd Pollock, a vaudeville theater owner out of Tarrytown, New York, who also used to work for the Miami Giants. Syd somehow got me confused with Buck O'Neal, so he started billing me as Buck O'Neil, and it stuck once the black newspapers picked up on it and began writing me up.

Nancy was also a case of mistaken identity, except it wasn't really a mistake—it was done on purpose. When Satchel and I were with the Monarchs, we played this one game on an Indian reservation near Sioux Falls, South Dakota. It was there that Satchel, who had a weakness for a pretty face, and the more of them the better, met this beautiful Indian maiden named Nancy, and since we were going to Chicago to play the Chicago American Giants, he invited Nancy to visit him there. She had some relatives there or something, so she accepted his invitation, and he told her we were staying at the Evans Hotel.

Well, now we were in Chicago, and I was sitting in the coffee shop of the Evans Hotel when I saw a cab pull up, and out stepped Nancy. I went out to greet her and tell her that Satchel was upstairs, and the bellhop carried her bags to his room.

A few minutes passed, and another cab pulled up, and this time out stepped Satchel's fiancée, Lahoma, who wasn't supposed to be coming by, as far as Satchel knew. Seeing how this might complicate things just a little bit, I jumped up and greeted her. "Lahoma," I said, "so *good* to see you. Satchel's not here right now, but he should be along shortly. Why don't you sit here with me, and I'll have the bellman take your bags up to the room."

I went over to the bellman, explained the situation to him, and told him to move Nancy and her bags into the room next to mine, which was also next door to Satchel's, and then to knock on Satchel's door and tell him Lahoma was here. A few minutes later, the bellman came down and gave me the sign that everything was okay. In the meantime, Satchel had climbed down the fire escape, and, lo and behold, there he came, walking down the street.

I said, "Look, Lahoma, here comes old Satchel now." Satch gave her a big greeting—"Lahoma, what a nice surprise!"—and led her upstairs.

That might have ended the trouble, except that later that night, after we had turned in, I heard Satchel's door open and close. Then I heard him knock on Nancy's door. I think he wanted to give her some money and apologize, but while he's whispering kind of loud, "Nancy! Nancy!" I hear *his* door open again, and I knew it was Lahoma coming out to see what was going on. I jumped out of my bed, opened my door, and said, "Yeah, Satch. What do you want?" And he said, "Why, Nancy. There you are. I was looking for you. What time is the game tomorrow?"

And from that night on, until his dying day, Satchel called me Nancy.

It was the Negro leagues that gave me an identity, but it was a lot more than just a nickname. I am proud to say it was the Negro leagues that turned me into a man. That's why this fame that's come my way so late in life is so funny to me. Thanks to Ken Burns, I became an overnight star in my eighties. But as far as I'm concerned, I felt like I was already on top of the world when I got to play with and against some of the best ballplayers who ever lived. In 1942, our Kansas City Monarchs beat the mighty Homestead Grays of Josh Gibson in the Negro World Series. I also met my wife Ora that year. That was a very good year. I never felt higher on top of the world than I did that year.

The big-leaguers might not have known who I was, but that was okay, because when I first thought of playing baseball for a living I never thought I would play major league baseball. I thought major league baseball was a white man's game. It was a thrill and a privilege to play against the big-leaguers in all-star games, and you know, we did pretty well

15

against those boys, and it made us believe we *did* belong up in the bigs.

But it just meant more to a black kid from the Deep South to know that millions of my people knew who I was. Believe you me, by the time those people were calling me Buck, I knew I had it made.

Chapter 2

Damn, There's Got to Be Something Better Than This

I am a black man named O'Neil. But I am also a descendant of the Mandingo tribe of western Africa.

My grandfather, Julius O'Neil, was a pure Mandingo, born on the banks of the Niger River, who was taken on a slave ship to America as a little boy. Julius worked on a plantation somewhere in the Carolinas, though more specific than that I cannot get because he didn't know himself just where those big cotton fields were. But he could clearly remember the man he worked for, a Mr. O'Neil, and it was the custom to take the surname of the man who owned you. So from then on, he was Mr. O'Neil, too, and so were his male descendants.

I was extremely fortunate to be able to know Julius O'Neil, who lived to be ninety-eight years old. When I was a kid and he was a very old man, I sat at his knee for hours with my mouth and my eyes wide open as he told me about working on the plantation for his master. But what I didn't expect to hear was that the O'Neils were good to him. Most people think of slave owners as Simon Legree, but Mr. O'Neil was a kind man who ran the whole show on his plantation, and he didn't bring in a tough overseer to whip the slaves because his kindness made them loyal to him.

Because of that, my grandfather wasn't a bitter man. He was an optimist. He thought black people could achieve any dream if they worked hard enough for it. He also thought there was enough good in any white man to overcome racism. I found out later on he was right about that, although I guess you'd have to say that as a society we've still got a ways to go.

When Julius was freed, he moved to southern Georgia, near the Florida border, and that's where my daddy, John Jordan O'Neil, grew up. He was a big, beautiful man. My mother, Luella, grew up in a town called Quincy, northwest of Tallahassee. She, too, was the child of slaves, although her ancestry was more mixed and her skin was lighter than my father's. I don't know the exact circumstances of their meeting, but I do know that I was born on November 13, 1911, in Carrabelle, a little fishing village on the Florida panhandle.

My father worked for a sawmill, operating the carriage, which is the machine that carries the logs through the saw blade that cuts them into lumber. It was a good job, as far as sawmill work goes, but my father was away from home a lot because the sawmills were portable. They would spend a few years cutting all the timber in a twenty- or thirty-square-mile area, then pack up the sawmill and move on to another spot. Papa would come home every other weekend, so my mother did most of the work raising me, my older sister Fanny, and my younger brother Warren.

It was when we were in Carrabelle that Julius O'Neil came to live with us one winter, and that's when I got to know him. Then he went to Jacksonville to live with his daughter, my aunt, just before he died. Julius left some long bloodlines. My father lived to be eighty-five. We Mr. O'Neils like to stick around a while.

My first memories of baseball came in Springdale, Florida, which is not too far from Carrabelle, where my father was working when I was five or six. He was a pretty good first baseman and a fine hitter, too, so he played on the local team on weekends. They didn't get any kind of salary, but they passed the hat through the stands and the players got a cut of what was collected. The only time they charged admission—ten cents or a quarter—was when a team from Pensacola or Tallahassee showed up. My father used to take me to the different little towns his team traveled to, and that's when I first started liking baseball. From then on, I played as much as I could.

Around 1920, my family moved to Sarasota, where the jobs were. The Ringling Brothers Circus had just moved from Indiana to Sarasota, and the women in my family, who were all good cooks, went to work cooking meals for the circus people. My mama was the cook for the Ringling family, the big bosses. She was hired by Ida Ringling North, who was John Ringling's sister. I suppose I could have gone to work for the circus; this was the age of the big top, and someone had to set up the big tents wherever the circus traveled, which is what a whole lot of black boys did in Sarasota when they got big enough. But that was as far as they could go in the circus. They weren't allowed to get up there on the trapeze, but they could sink those spikes into the ground and hope the circus would take them from town to town—a life that, when you think about it, isn't all that different from the life of a baseball player. And, believe me, there were some moments in my career when I felt I was in a circus. But that's for later.

Although my mother worked for circus people and we had a great deal of affection for the Ringlings, who were fine people, she wanted me to stay away from that life. The men who went around with the circus made pretty good money, but they were older men. They were kind of rough and tumble. Every night was a one-night stand. She didn't want me to be in that unrooted atmosphere, and she herself wasn't satisfied as a cook for someone's family. Eventually she put down her own roots when she and my father opened their own restaurant in Sarasota. They called it O'Neil's, which made us proud. (Recently, I had something named after *me,* but again I'm getting ahead of myself.)

Anyway, Mama was a woman of many talents. She could cook, she could sing, she could even make a pretty good baseball out of socks wrapped around a rock. We could buy balls in the store for a quarter, but a quarter was a lot of money, and anyway, Mama's baseballs lasted longer than the store-bought ones, with their cottonseed cores.

We moved to Sarasota for the work, but it turns out we got closer to baseball, too. A lot of the major league teams had spring training in that area. John McGraw and the New York Giants trained right in town. Connie Mack and the Philadelphia Athletics were down in Fort Myers, and Miller Huggins and the

New York Yankees were up in Tampa and then St. Petersburg. We especially liked for the Yankees to come to town, because they would hit that ball over the fence like nobody's business, and I guess I'm one of the few people still around who can say he saw Babe Ruth hit a home run. Us black kids, of course, were waiting on the other side of the fence; we'd sell those balls to tourists and maybe keep one or two for ourselves.

Later on, I would be fortunate enough to meet Ruth and a lot of the other big-leaguers personally. I met Lefty Grove and the Dean brothers, Dizzy and Daffy. I saw John McGraw and Connie Mack managing. As a student of the game, I admired men like Jimmie Foxx, Herb Pennock, and Lou Gehrig, and it was a great thrill and privilege to play against some of them in black-versus-white all-star games between our regular Negro league ballgames. But, you know, there was something different about that side of the baseball world. As I told you, I never thought I would play major league ball. It wasn't like I felt deprived; it was just understood that big-league baseball was white baseball.

Black baseball, on the other hand, was relevant to our lives. We read about it in the *Chicago Defender* or the *Amsterdam News* or the *Pittsburgh Courier;* my father subscribed to those weekly papers mostly so I could learn about the Negro baseball teams. When the mail arrived on Monday, all the kids were at my house, reading about Dick Lundy, who was from Jacksonville and was a great shortstop with the Bacharach Giants of Atlantic City. Or the legendary John Henry Lloyd, another fantastic shortstop from Palatka, Florida. We called him Pop; the Cubans called him *El Cuchara*—the Tablespoon—because he "set the table" by getting on base all the time, and Babe Ruth once called him the greatest player of all time when Lloyd was playing for and managing the New York Lincoln Giants and many other teams. We read about these guys until we wore the paper out, then we'd go out and make believe we were Pop Lloyd and Dick Lundy until it got too dark to see the ball.

In the winter of 1923, I got to see some of the men I had been reading about. My father's brother, Uncle Handy, lived up in New York City, in Harlem, and worked as a porter on the railroad running between New York and Miami. That winter he came by Sarasota and picked up my father and me and took us across the state to West Palm Beach.

Now, there were two fancy hotels across the channel in Palm Beach, the Royal Poinciana and the Breakers. Some of the wealthiest people in the country flocked there in the winter, but so did hundreds of black workers, including some who played for two of the best teams in black baseball, the Chicago American Giants and the Indianapolis ABCs. Those players were not exactly lounging on the beach or playing golf like players do nowadays. They worked at the hotels over those winter months as bellhops, waiters, cooks, chauffeurs. Each hotel sponsored a baseball team as entertainment for the help, although some of the tourists occasionally showed up to watch them play, too. The Giants represented the Royal Poinciana and the ABCs were the Breakers' house team, and for four months of the year, on Sundays and for half a day on Thursdays, when the help was off, some of the best baseball in the country was played in Palm Beach.

And it wasn't like white baseball, either. While the major leagues relied on the longball that Babe Ruth brought to the game, black baseball was fast and aggressive, with lots of stealing, bunting, hit-and-run play. It was the game Jackie Robinson learned and then brought to the majors twenty-four years later—speed, intelligence, unbridled aggressiveness on the basepaths—and for a twelve-year-old boy from Sarasota, it was *thrilling*.

I saw Speed Boy Reese and Bingo DeMoss and Jelly Gardner and Biz Mackey—who taught Roy Campanella how to catch—and a submariner named Dizzy Dismukes, who would one day become my mentor. I also saw the greatest player I have ever seen in eight-and-a-third decades, and one of the greatest men.

That player was Oscar Charleston, who was at that time the centerfielder for the ABCs. To this day, I always claim that Willie Mays was the greatest major league player I have ever seen . . . but then I pause and say that Oscar Charleston was even better. Charlie was a tremendous left-handed hitter, but he could also bunt, steal a hundred bases a year, and cover center field as well as anyone before him or after. Why, in sixty games in 1921, they said he hit .434 with fifteen home runs and thirty-five stolen bases, which would be something like forty homers and ninety-five steals in a full major league season. He was like Ty Cobb, Babe Ruth, and Tris Speaker rolled into one. He was a big man with a temper like a flytrap, and he was always getting into fights with players, umpires, and fans. I learned later that you always wanted to stay on his good side.

Another great man I saw that winter in Palm Beach was none other than Andrew "Rube" Foster, who's often called the father of black baseball, although he came along after black baseball had been around for fifty years. But it fits, because Rube Foster *was* black baseball starting in the early part of this century.

I could write a book about Rube. They say he was the best pitcher of his day, when he was throwing no-hitters all the time for the Philadelphia Giants and Cuban X-Giants around the turn of the century. But it's what he did off the field that's truly significant. A brilliant strategist and scout, they say he was a secret advisor to John McGraw, and that he taught McGraw's top pitcher, Christy Mathewson, how to throw the screwball—only they called it the fadeaway back then. Rube also invented the hit-and-run, although he called it the bunt-and-run. He would have his grounds-keepers let the infield grass grow high and pack the baselines with mud to keep the bunts in fair ground, and while they'd be rolling the base runners would be flying around the bases.

When Rube went to the Chicago Giants in 1910, he renamed the team the Chicago American Giants. Rube named it that for a reason: He wanted it to be a national team, as a way of selling black baseball. He took the team on tours throughout the South so that black folks down there could see a great attraction. For us, seeing the Chicago American Giants in their red-and-white uniforms and CAG across their shirts, it was like seeing the gods come down from heaven. Truth is, for me, it was like seeing my future.

Only a man like Rube, with his genius and ambition, could have established the Negro National League in 1920. He was so astute and so far ahead of his time. He thought that if he'd organize black baseball, then one day the major leagues would take in a black team. Baseball didn't expand until 1962, but Rube was thinking expansion in 1920.

Now, that was a daring thing to dream, and unfortunately he was just too far ahead of his time. The Negro National League outlived Rube, who drove himself to exhaustion building up the league and met a sad end, dying in a mental institution in Kankakee, Illinois, in 1930. To give you some idea of what Rube Foster meant to us, people filed past his casket for three days after his funeral in Chicago, which was one of the largest funerals ever to take place there.

When I first saw him, Rube was well past his prime as a pitcher, but he was still a showman, baffling the hitters with a lot of changeups. He was something to watch even in the dugout. He smoked a meerschaum pipe and signaled his players and coaches with smoke rings. *Smoke rings!* I spent a lot of time trying to figure out his system, but I couldn't. Maybe they were decoys one day or one game or one inning, and not another. Who knows? Rube was way ahead of his time in the psychological side of the game—we didn't even know there was one. He was always trying to fool the other team, and most of the time he did. I admired him so much that, because of him, I wanted to be a manager one day.

Come to think of it, that was a pretty silly ambition

for a twelve-year-old. But I was baseball crazy, and people like Rube Foster gave me the idea that it was possible to dream the dream of playing for a living. I was already a pretty good player. There was a semipro team in our town—the Sarasota Tigers—and most of the men on that team had sons playing on our grammar school team. The Tigers used the field at our school, so they saw the end of our practices as they were getting ready to start theirs.

One day the manager of the Tigers came by my school to talk to Miss Emma Booker, our principal. His first baseman was ill and couldn't play in the game that Thursday afternoon, so he asked her if I could get out a little early and fill in. I was only twelve years old, but they were already starting to call me Foots because of my big feet, and I was pretty good, if I do say so myself. I did a nice job for the Tigers that day, and pretty soon I took over for the older guy.

It's funny, but I never left first base for another thirty years. I had a decent arm, so I could have been an outfielder, but I looked like a first baseman, so a first baseman I became. I played with the Tigers for two seasons, and I had the time of my life. We played mostly on weekends because the men had regular jobs, and we traveled all over the state, to Tampa, St. Pete, Miami, West Palm. We played what we called PC, or percentage baseball. That didn't refer to a strategy; it meant there was a 60-40 split of the gate receipts, with the winning team getting the 60 percent. Out of each team's share, the manager got 20 percent, and the players split up the rest.

Because the Tigers were owned by a man named Henry Winn, who owned the Colson Hotel in town, we would spend the night in the hotel before travel days, which started very early in the morning. This was pretty exciting stuff for a twelve-year-old—I was by far the youngest player on the team—but the other guys were very protective of me. After the ballgame, they would have a few drinks and do a lot of other things I could only guess at, but they wouldn't let me do anything.

My father had to stop playing baseball after an accident where he lost his big toe in the sawmill—the blade went right through his shoe. But he still worked after that, clearing land near Sarasota, working as a foreman on the celery farm. Papa was a very friendly man. He respected people, and he was respected in return. He even had some white friends, which was almost unheard of at the time. He didn't grovel in front of them; he was just outgoing.

Sarasota was better than most towns in Florida for black folks. Jim Crow was still very much alive, and we had no high school, and my father couldn't vote even though he had to pay taxes. We could only sit in the balcony at the movie theater, but that was just an inconvenience. Sometimes, if the roads needed maintenance, the county would round up as many young black men as they needed, charge them with vagrancy, and put them on chain gangs for a few months. But at least the Ku Klux Klan wasn't around, not like it was a few miles away in Manatee County, where they actually had lynchings.

Still, no black family was immune from injustice. Our brush with prejudice came one night at O'Neil's. After the restaurant had stopped serving, a white deputy sheriff went around back into the kitchen, where my mother was talking with some friends. My father had been out front, doing the same thing with his friends, but when he saw that deputy go around to the back he wondered what he was up to and followed him.

Without knocking, the deputy opened the kitchen door and waltzed right in. Mama demanded of him, "Mister, what are you doing in my kitchen?" Everything got real quiet, and the deputy sheriff's face turned beet red. For a black person to even look a white deputy sheriff in the eye was considered uppity, and to confront him with a question was practically a crime—an even bigger crime if you were a black woman. The deputy raised his hand to hit Mama, but my father was right behind him. He grabbed the deputy's arm, punched him right in the face, and sent him sprawling across the table. Mama's friends scattered like they were birds.

I'm just glad that deputy didn't strike my mother. If he had, I do believe Papa would have killed him without even thinking about it. After he hit him, he did think about it, and he realized he had to get out of town. He hid at a friend's house, and that night one of his Masonic Lodge brothers drove him to Tampa, where he caught a train to New York City to stay with my Uncle Handy. Handy worked for the railroad, but he also owned a little poolroom, and my father helped him run it while he waited for things to cool off. As it turned out, that deputy must have had a bad reputation, because the sheriff told my mother that he could have smoothed things over had we gone to him first. 'Course, my father didn't know that at the time, and he wasn't about to take any chances, even after we told him it was okay to come back home. So we didn't see him for several years.

Besides my mother and my father, and the AME Church in Carrabelle—I was crawling in front of the altar there when I was a kid, while the pastor was giving his sermon—I was blessed with one other guiding light. That was the principal of my elementary school, Emma Booker, whom I've already mentioned. Miss Booker—that's what I always called her, Miss

Booker, even years and years later—was a tall, strik-ing woman and maybe the most intelligent person in all of Sarasota. She was really something. Miss Booker got her degree at a colored school, Spellman College in Atlanta, but she couldn't get her master's degree in the South, so she went all the way up to Columbia University in New York to get it. Then, having been taught by some of the finest educators in the world, she came back to Sarasota to dedicate her life to us.

If you go to Sarasota today, you'll find a Booker Elementary School, a Booker Junior High School, and a Booker High School. That's how much she meant to kids in Sarasota. She used to buy us books out of her own pocket. Because she knew that eighth grade was as far as most of us were going, she had summer classes for us. Geography was big with Miss Booker; she wanted us to know something about the world, even if most of us weren't going to see very much of it. She wanted us to dream our dreams, and then to go out and try and live them.

Actually, I was more fortunate than most kids in that I was able to spend the summer vacation in New York City, in Harlem, one year, an experience I'll tell you about in a bit. So I knew how exciting the world was outside Sarasota. But other than that, about the only geography I was familiar with was the celery fields just outside of town. And they were anything but exciting.

When you go to a grocery store or a cocktail party, you probably don't think too much about how that nice, crisp celery got there. As a teenager who used to help bring that celery to the table, let me tell you. Celery grows in the muck and gets harvested in dirt so oven-hot it makes you itch. It's miserable work. First, a man pushes a plow along the row and cuts the celery about an inch below the ground. Then other people, mostly women, come along and strip off the bad leaves. Then the box boys, which is what I was, follow along behind the women and place empty crates along the rows. A crew following us packs the celery in the crates, and then a truck comes along to pick up the crates and take them to a building where the celery is washed and packed for shipping.

Most box boys would carry a box in each hand, but because I was tall and strong, I could put one box on top of the other and carry four. So I was considered a good box boy. That entitled me to make the princely sum of $1.25 a day.

I did that for three seasons. One day in the third year, toward the end of the harvest, the foreman blew the whistle for lunch. I had been doing nothing but carrying boxes for weeks, and it was even hotter than usual and so humid that it felt like we were working in a steam bath. There was this big stack of boxes on the ground. On one side of the boxes sat my father, who was a foreman on the farm, eating lunch with some of the older men. On the other side sat seventeen-year-old J. J. O'Neil, tired and probably a little delirious from the heat. The thought of working on the celery harvest every autumn for the rest of my life was more than I could stand. So I said to myself— out loud, mind you—"Damn, there has *got* to be something better than this."

That night, after the truck that took us from the fields to the town dropped us off, my father and I were walking home when he said, "Jay, I heard what you said today at lunch." I thought he was going to reprimand me for swearing. But what he said was, "You're right. There *is* something better than this. But you can't find it here. You're going to have to go out and get it."

The big problem was how to do that. I wanted to go to college someday, but like I said, in Florida there were only four high schools for black kids in the whole state, in Miami, Jacksonville, Pensacola, and Tampa. When I finished eighth grade, there wasn't any school for me to go to. See, the powers that be thought, well, that's all the education black kids needed because a black kid was just going to go work on the farm or be a porter or a bellman at the hotels or a dishwasher or a shoeshine boy. But to know that your education stopped when you were fourteen, and all that was out there was celery or the blade of a sawmill or the shoes of a white man, well, it didn't seem right, and I didn't think it was enough.

As it happened, luck was on my side. I had a friend named Lloyd Haisley, who had graduated from Edward Waters College, a small Methodist school in Jacksonville. Waters was like Florida A&M, and it had a high school department for black kids from all across Florida. Lloyd introduced me to Ox Clemons, the baseball and football coach at Waters, and he gave me a scholarship.

And that was the jumpoff point for me. Still, looking back almost seventy years later, I find myself thinking about where I came from. Little things take me back. In 1994, when the owners and players were arguing over a salary cap, I saw this fan with a stalk of celery on his head that he called a celery cap. I had to laugh. If it hadn't been for people like Emma Booker and Lloyd Haisley, and for baseball, I might've fallen victim seventy years ago to a celery cap of my own.

Chapter 3

I Ate So Much
My Mama Cried

One of the added benefits of appearing in Ken Burns's *Baseball,* besides being discovered and all, was that I got a chance to visit some of my old stompin' grounds. Ken and Lynn Novick, the lovely producer who first interviewed me for the series, invited me to come down to Orlando to talk to some of those nice PBS folks, and one day Lynn and I took a little side trip over to Daytona Beach, which is where my niece Sally Griffin still lives. In that one afternoon, I just about relived my whole baseball career.

Bethune-Cookman College, in Daytona, was one of our arch rivals when I played at Edward Waters. I

could still see Ox Clemons standing there on the sidelines, a big barrel-chested man who was built a lot like
Babe Ruth. We went over to what used to be known as
City Island Park but is now called Jackie Robinson
Ballpark, because that's where Jackie first integrated
organized baseball, playing as a member of the 1946
Montreal Royals in the Brooklyn Dodgers' farm system. The man there said the park was fifty-five years
old, but I had to correct him: I played there in 1934
with the Miami Giants.

Sixty years disappeared just like that, and I was on
first base warming up the other infielders: Ollie "the
Ghost" Marcelle at third, Bill Riggins at short, Winky
James at second. Over there, back behind the tool shed
along the right field line, that's where the colored folks
had to sit.

I visited with Sally for a while, and she showed me
my old report card from elementary school that her
mother and my sister Fanny had passed on to her. I'm
proud to say I got mostly As, including one in personal hygiene. On the way out of town, we stopped by
another field where some kids, black and white, boy
and girl, were playing kickball. The scout in me noticed that the best player was a girl—she could fly!
The old man in me thought that a game like that would
not have been possible the last time I was there.

That was in 1952. On that same field, I managed the

Kansas City Monarchs in an exhibition game against the Indianapolis Clowns. You might've heard of the two shortstops who played that day. Ours was Ernie Banks. Theirs was Henry Aaron.

They were just at the beginnings of their journeys then. About twenty-three years earlier, my own journey began, on the ballfield at Edward Waters College. When I got there, I strolled onto the field, ready to be anointed as the new first baseman. But was I in for a surprise! There were other kids just as good as me, and I had to scuffle. Even after I had established myself, new players would come along who wanted my position. We were a college team, but we used to play against outstanding—and cutthroat—semipro teams like the Jacksonville Red Caps, who were guys who worked as redcaps, or porters, at the railroad terminal. Some of my teammates spent their summers playing for the New York Black Yankees, who played in the Negro National League. People don't realize the Negro leagues were filled with college men, maybe more than were in the white big leagues.

Going to Edward Waters was an education in life and baseball. Ox Clemons was like a professor of baseball; he taught me the basics. We kids had just *played* baseball; we didn't know too much about the fundamentals. For example, I never knew anything about the hit-and-run. I didn't know anything about hitting behind the runner. A lot of black teams used the bunt-and-run, Rube Foster's favorite play. And old Ox, he would tell us, if the first baseman and the third base-man are coming in and crowding you looking for the bunt, take a half-swing and punch the ball over their heads. If you could, what with the baserunners all on the move, it would be like a carousel turning.

I didn't know hitting was so scientific! But fielding was like that, too, as I learned. Ox taught me how to come off first base. I used to dash off the bag while holding a runner on, to get into position to field the ball, but he told me to kinda trail out there, so I could stop and be able to come back if the ball was hit behind me. This is what the great first basemen do, and I was doing it at age fourteen!

Professor Ox also taught me about life. Watching him, I learned how to be tough, how to fight and survive, but also how to handle people. I had always been able to get along with people, but Ox showed me that everybody has a different personality and you can't treat all people the same way. Some you've got to stroke, some you've got to challenge to get the best out of them. But the most important rule was that every player on a team was equal. That rule stayed with me through the years. When I played, I treated the rookies like I did the older guys. Actually, I might have had a little more patience with rookies, and that helped me as a manager. When you're managing, you're trying to handle a lot of young guys away from home for the first time. You have to be Daddy as well as manager.

I spent four years at Edward Waters, two for high school (after tests, I was promoted to the eleventh grade) and two for college, and while I still regret not getting my college diploma, I do believe I got an *education.* But I also realized it was now or never as far as baseball was concerned. Along about 1933 I hooked up with my first professional team, the Tampa Black Smokers, and I left home, traveling all the way to southern Georgia. After about a month with the Smokers, I got an offer to join the Miami Giants.

It seems like half the teams in black baseball were called the Giants. There were the Bacharach Giants, the Lincoln Giants, the Brooklyn Royal Giants, the Brooklyn Cuban Giants, the Cuban X Giants, the Philadelphia Giants, the Pittsburgh Giants, the Chicago Giants, the Chicago American Giants, Cole's American Giants, Gilkerson's Union Giants, the Celeron Acme Colored Giants, the Shreveport Acme Giants, the Page Fence Giants, the St. Louis Giants, the Harrisburg Giants, the Mohawk Giants, the Baltimore Elite Giants, the Columbus Elite Giants, the Columbia Giants, the Twin City Giants, the Quaker Giants of New York, the Zulu Cannibal Giants . . . among others.

The reason there were so many Giants was that many newspapers across the country refused to print pictures of black people. But there were a lot of excellent black teams around, and they were a big attraction, even in predominantly white towns. So Giants became a code word. If you saw a placard in a store window or an advertisement in the newspaper announcing that the River City Giants were coming to town to play the local semipro team, you knew right away that the visiting team was a black one. I think everybody in the Negro leagues was a Giant at least once. I was a Giant three times!

Now, the Miami Giants happened to have been owned by two bootleggers, Johnny Pierce and, as I mentioned before, a man named Buck O'Neal. You couldn't afford to be too picky about whom you played for, because a lot of clubs were owned by men who ran numbers rackets and booze. In those days, guys like that could afford to run a team better than other black businessmen. Our manager was Wayne Carr, who was a pretty good pitcher at one time and had seen me with the Sarasota Tigers. The Miami Giants were sort of an unofficial minor league team of the Negro National League—not Rube Foster's league, mind you, but the one that started up in 1932 in the East—and though there were no formal agreements, we supplied younger players to the big clubs.

For the first time in my life, I actually got a salary for playing baseball: ten dollars a week, plus room and board. We stayed in a hotel over a theater on Second Avenue, and I could look down onto the street and see the sidewalks crowded with black folks. That was thrilling enough for a country boy from Florida, but was nothing compared to our road trip to New York City, which actually was a return trip for me, and one I'd been looking forward to for years, ever since I went to visit Uncle Handy when I was fourteen.

That's the trip I was telling you about before, after I had graduated from Emma Booker's school, and, man, I came away from it thinking that Harlem was just like what I imagined heaven would be. So many people, so many *black* people, and a lifetime of treasures. I had ridden up there with Uncle Handy, and I had stayed with him for the summer. You can imagine what Harlem represented to a fourteen-year-old boy from the Deep South. Any black kid in the world would have had to have heard of Harlem. I learned a lot hearing the circus guys talk about it. And of course Miss Booker used to tell us about the great writers of the Harlem Renaissance, like Langston Hughes, and the great musicians like blues singer Bessie Smith and jazz trumpet player Louis Armstrong. I heard them all because my parents would play records on the big old

Victrola in our living room, with the big horn speaker and all.

Uncle Handy lived in a walkup apartment on 128th Street and Lenox Avenue, right behind the Apollo Theater—and you better believe I went to see show-time at the Apollo. Me and everybody else in town. Uncle Handy knew all the places to go. But to me, Harlem was more than great attractions. It was a state of mind. In Sarasota, you knew your place. But in Harlem, I didn't know anything about segregation. When I got there, I rode the subways and streetcars and I could sit anyplace I wanted to. I didn't have to go to the back seat or back door for nothing.

It's funny. I thought I was hip to what was happening as a kid. I had me a couple of suits and I thought for sure I was looking good. When I got to Harlem that summer, man, the kids weren't wearing the kind of suit I had on—and my suits were new! So I took my suits to the pawnbroker there on 125th Street and I told him, I said, "Mister, will you take my two suits and give me one like these boys are wearing?" And he did. He gave me a zoot suit, the kind made famous by Cab Calloway, with the big flaps down the back. I wore it and then I took it home to Sarasota and wore it some more. I remember it so well: Oxford gray. Wide at the shoulders and tight at the hips. Made me feel like a movie star.

Well, I didn't have that suit when I went back up north with the Miami Giants, but I knew where to go to get one. Because now I was a man, twenty-three years old, and for a man Harlem had added meaning. You had to look good for the ladies, like you knew what you were doing. So when we left Sarasota, I was the guy in charge of telling these older guys about Harlem. It took us two weeks in two old jalopies to get from Florida up to there, playing our way up by day and driving at night. And when we got to Harlem, we stayed at the Woodside Hotel, which was another dream come true.

The Woodside was where all the black ballteams stayed. The big bands, too. That was a jumping joint, a lot of action, and Count Basie immortalized it in his song "Jumpin' at the Woodside." Down through the years I must have seen just about all of the great black musicians come and go through the lobby. It was always jumpin' at the Woodside.

But the most wonderful part of that trip was going to Yankee Stadium for the first time to watch the New York Black Yankees and the New York Cubans play in a four-team Negro league doubleheader. Black baseball was a matter of great pride in the black community, and it was important for black celebrities to be associated with the game. Fact is, you could say Negro league ball was one of the black arts, like jazz and the blues. Louis Armstrong owned his own team in New Orleans, the Smart Nine, and the Black Yankees were owned by Bill "Bojangles" Robinson, the greatest tap dancer of them all, who played in all those Shirley Temple movies.

The fans in New York came by the thousands to see these teams, and their favorite player was David "Showboat" Thomas, the flashiest first baseman I have ever seen. The Cubans had the great Martin Dihigo, the only player to be elected to the Mexican, Cuban, and American Baseball Halls of Fame. I later found out that one of the pitchers for the Cubans was a left-hander named Luis Tiant, the father of the Luis Tiant who went through all those wild gyrations on the mound and pitched in the World Series for the Boston Red Sox.

One of my teammates with the Miami Giants was Oliver Marcelle, who in his prime was one of the best third basemen in the game. We called Ollie the Ghost, because he was something of a loner on the road. He'd disappear after the games were over, and then he'd show up when we were ready for the next one; we'd see him and say, "Well, here comes the Ghost!" He was a Creole from New Orleans, a handsome man who took pride in his looks. But he was also a hot-tempered individual. One winter in Cuba, Ollie got into a fight during a crap game, and he got the end of his nose bit off by Frank Warfield, another veteran black ballplayer who once managed the Lincoln Giants. For the rest of his life, this good-looking man had to go around with a piece of tape on his nose.

You get the idea by now that a man couldn't be a weakling in our leagues. We had the scars to prove it, only not quite as bad as Ollie's. As tough as Ollie Marcelle was, though, I heard a story passed along recently that sounds like it needs some straightening out. Somebody said Ollie hit Oscar Charleston over the head with a bat. Remember, I told you about Oscar. Now, Ollie was a tough man, but I have to think that if he hit big Oscar with a bat, Oscar would have broken that bat and killed him with it. Oscar had a stoplight nailed to his chest. You didn't cross him.

Our shortstop was Bill Riggins, and he, too, was past his best days. Bill had a little drinking problem that sometimes interfered with his performance. But together with Wayne Carr, Ollie and Bill talked me into joining their new traveling team, the New York Tigers. Now, we had nothing to do with New York, but we figured the name would get us some attention from the people fascinated with Harlem. (The Harlem Globetrotters, organized and based in Chicago, had pretty much decided the same thing.) Out West where we were headed, nobody was going to know the difference.

'Course, we were also headed out into the Depression. We left Sarasota that spring in these two old seven-passenger cars, Cadillacs with jump seats in them, one of which my father had bought for a hundred dollars. Those were the same kind of cars we had gone to New York in, and you could get cars like that for very little money. The people who sold them just wanted to get them off the lot, they were so old. Doby Major, a friend of mine from Sarasota, joined us, and off we went seeking fame and fortune.

It started out okay. One of our first stops was Monroe, Louisiana, which is where the famous Pittsburgh Crawfords spent spring training. They were owned by the notorious Gus Greenlee, a big, cigar-chomping numbers man who owned the hottest nightclub in Pittsburgh, the Crawford Grille, on Bedford Avenue in the Hill section. The team Greenlee put together—he could buy the best players around—had Satchel Paige, Oscar Charleston, Cool Papa Bell, Judy Johnson, and Josh Gibson.

They were there in Monroe with that big luxurious Mack bus they went around the country in. Marcelle and Riggins knew them all, so that gave us younger players entrée. Sometimes we would talk to them, but mostly we sat around with our mouths open listening to the stories they told. A lot of the talk was about Satchel, who hadn't gotten to Monroe because he was still in Cuba or someplace pitching for one team or another. That's what he would do, pitch for whoever would pay him, and because Gus knew he couldn't stop him, he would rent Satchel out to other ballclubs in the States during the Negro league season. He'd come in on Sunday, then he'd be gone, playing someplace else for much of the week. By doing this, Gus could get a split of some of that money Satchel would bring home.

But in 1934, Satchel and Gus had a falling out over money, and that's what the ballplayers were all abuzz about, that Satchel wasn't going to come in. They were right, too, because he wound up jumping the Crawfords that season and playing for an integrated semi-pro team out in Bismarck, North Dakota. That team, by the way, also had other Negro league greats like Quincy Trouppe, Ted Radcliffe, and Chet Brewer on it, playing right along with white ballplayers with no problems at all, and that was a real landmark for our game. I know how great that team was, because we would meet up with them along the way.

The interesting thing about how the guys talked about Satchel was that they were happy that he was making the big money. A lot of people thought the Negro league ballplayers were jealous of him, but the truth was that we all wanted to join up with Satchel, because on those barnstorming tours we would go on, when Negro league all-stars played teams headed up by Dizzy Dean or Bob Feller, guys could make more money in thirty days than they made all season. Satchel was a money tree for all of us, and for our game.

Gus didn't begrudge anybody making some money. Josh Gibson was also late to report to Monroe, because he, too, was in Cuba, playing in Havana or San Fuego. See, if you were good enough, you'd get invited down there to the Latin-American countries over the winter and make good money. But I did get to see Josh a little later. Let me tell you, Josh Gibson was a big, beautiful man. Great shoulders, small in the waist. And, Lord, he hit that ball! In 1935, he was at his peak, and he was one of the nicest men I've ever known. They say he had a lot of problems, but I never saw him any different, never saw him change, not until he got very sick later on, and even then he was the most popular ballplayer black baseball ever had.

But, tell you what, Cool Papa Bell wasn't too far behind. Everywhere he went, people would want to know about Cool Papa and how fast he was, because there were so many stories about him scoring from first base on a single or stealing home. And Cool would be like a one-man clinic, sitting out on the porch behind the rooming house talking about baseball. He'd talk about the different guys he'd seen steal in the old days and where he picked up this move or how the toughest guy to hit against was Bullet Joe Rogan, and so on.

Later, when I got to see Cool Papa play, I knew that what everybody said about him was dead-on true. When Jesse Owens got back from winning his gold medals at the 1936 Olympics in Berlin, Gus Greenlee hired him to run races against horses around the bases before games to entertain the crowd. And Jesse would also race the ballplayers sometimes. He'd give guys a ten-yard head start and still beat them every time. But I don't ever remember him racing Cool Papa. I don't think he wanted to take that chance.

Boy, wouldn't that have been something—Jesse Owens racing against Cool Papa Bell! I'll say this, going from first to home, Jesse wouldn't have beaten Cool Papa. Cool Papa was the fastest man I've ever seen. He was faster than Maury Wills and Lou Brock and Mickey Mantle when Mickey had good legs. He was faster than Bo Jackson and Kenny Lofton. But more than that, baserunning isn't only about speed. It's about technique, cutting the corners and keeping your balance. And Cool Papa, he was a master at all of that.

So this was how it was when the great players sat around: The talk was all baseball. Baseball was our life, and people like Cool Papa and Oscar Charleston would pass down the tradition from one generation to the next. Later on, I'd be doing the same thing.

Learning about my heroes and playing ball, that was the good part of those early days on the road. The bad part was living hand to mouth. Our booking agents were only getting us a game or two a week, and that just wasn't enough to keep up with the expenses. We were lucky that we could live pretty cheap; because of Jim Crow laws, we couldn't stay at the hotels, so we stayed in rooming houses that we knew from other guys were okay. All the towns had them, and I still have the black book I used to keep—like all the black ballplayers used to keep—listing all the rooming houses down south. This was part of the tradition, too. We'd share this information about where you could stay, where you could get a good meal, where the softest beds were. Everything you'd need to know.

Only thing is, in Monroe we fell so far behind with the rent, we couldn't pay the landlady. So she said, "Here's what I'll do. I'll take one of your cars until you can pay me and come back and get the car." Well, we didn't ever get back. We went off to Shreveport and we didn't have but the one car, and we had eleven ballplayers. So what we did was, we put three guys into the front seat, three more in the jump seat, three in the back seat, and two guys out on the running boards. You know, cars back then had big running boards along the sides. One guy standing on the left would stick out his right arm and a guy standing on the right would stick out his left arm—and they'd hold each other across the top of the car. And after you would go about 250 miles, you'd stop and two other guys would come out and the two on the running boards would come in. We'd rotate that way.

While we were in Shreveport, Ralph Jones, who was the baseball coach at Grambling (and later the president of the college), invited us to come out for the day to play his ballclub in exchange for free meals, and we leaped at the opportunity. But, again, we couldn't pay the bill at our rooming house. So we all snuck out the back window in the middle of the night. But I wouldn't go until I left a note promising to pay the landlady, and as soon as I was able to, I mailed her the money.

I know what you're thinking, that this sure sounds a lot like the *Bingo Long* story. And it was. It was a lot like a circus act. Man, I was starting to think I had joined Ringling Brothers after all. But I'll say again, too many people think this was what Negro league baseball was like. It wasn't. It was what we had to do when we were out barnstorming. Heck, I hoboed on that trip, too. Caught a freight train. That was when we lost the automobile. It just died on us, and we had to get to Wichita Falls, Texas, to play a team there called the Black Spudders—this was potato country, you see—on June 19.

That's an important date. The nineteenth of June is celebrated by the blacks in the South as Emancipation Day, the day in 1863 when the last slaves in west Texas were notified of their freedom. It was to be our Emancipation Day, too, because the Black Spudders always drew a big crowd on June 19. We were already counting on the money.

What we weren't counting on was the weather. The Spudders had been in San Antonio a few days before, and it rained so hard on their way back that a river somewhere between San Antonio and Wichita Falls flooded. They couldn't get across until it receded, and that was a few days after Emancipation Day. We eventually played the game, but we got nowhere near the crowd we would have gotten. After the game, we had about forty cents among us.

Fortunately, I had another skill. Back in Sarasota, there was a poolroom next to my mother's restaurant, and I would go in after the place was closed and clean up and brush the tables. A lot of nights, after I finished the chores, I stayed and shot a few racks, and I got to be a fair country pool player. When we got stranded in Wichita Falls, I collected the little bit of money we had and started playing some nine-ball. I did pretty well, too. With the four or five dollars I made, we bought some groceries—beans, rice, cornmeal, bread, white pork.

Thus fortified, we probably all should have headed back home. But there was an annual semipro tournament in Denver sponsored by the *Denver Post,* and the Kansas City Monarchs had paved the way for black teams to play in it back in the twenties, which the sponsors liked because this stirred up excitement. You know, it's not generally known that out in the heartland and in the West, black baseball had a good base of white fans. Those people out there, who had no big-league teams of their own, knew there was another "big-league" level of baseball around, and they loved to come watch black teams. And I have to believe that helped ease the path for integration in the big leagues, because the big-league owners saw how many fans were aware of this other game out there.

Anyway, about that *Denver Post* tournament, the manager of the Black Spudders, who were headed up there themselves, found out that there was a man in Denver named Joe Alpert who wanted a black ballclub to represent his clothing store. Wayne Carr got him on the phone and Mr. Alpert agreed to sponsor us—if we could get to Denver. No problem, Wayne said.

The problem was, we now had no car. The Spudders were kind enough to pack six of our older players and all our equipment in one of their cars. The rest of us hopped another freight train out of Wichita Falls for the twenty-four-hour ride to Denver. Since hobos were a common sight in the Depression, we didn't have any trouble.

We pulled into Denver early in the morning, stiff and tired but happy to be there. After Wayne met us, we had breakfast on the soup line—every train station had one—cleaned ourselves up, and called Mr. Alpert. He picked us up and put us up in a big house in the black neighborhood called Five Points. The New York Tigers were now the Joe Alpert Clothiers, and we got Mr. Alpert a little extra publicity, and ourselves a little money, by beating four teams. We lost before we got to the finals, which paid the winner five thousand dollars, but we ended up with about two hundred.

Now all we wanted to do was buy a car and get back to Florida. But we also heard about a new tournament in Wichita, Kansas, called the National Baseball Congress tournament. You might have heard about it because it's still being played, but back in '35 it was brand-new, and the organizers wanted as many teams as they could get—even black teams. Besides, it was on our way home, so to speak. Wayne found a man in Denver who was such a baseball fan that he offered to drive all of us all the way to Wichita in his seven-passenger car. We were the New York Tigers again.

We got all the way to the semifinals, where we lost

to a team from Duncan, Oklahoma, called the Duncan Cementers. This is where we met up with Satchel's Bismarck team. Bismarck had been winning everything in sight that fall—including the *Denver Post* tournament we'd been knocked out of. Then they came to Wichita and rampaged through that tournament. That had been the master plan of a Bismarck car dealer named Neil Churchill, who wanted to assemble the best team he could regardless of color. So, as I said before, he went out and got Satchel, who was arguing with Gus Greenlee over money, as well as Ted Radcliffe—who was known as Double Duty after the newspaperman Damon Runyon saw him pitch one end of a doubleheader and then catch Satchel in the other. Churchill also got pitchers Chet Brewer and Hilton Smith and outfielder Quincy Trouppe.

I had heard of Satchel, of course, from one end of the country to the other, but this was the first time I ever got to shake hands with him. He turned out to be very friendly, very approachable, even though he was a big star. He loved an audience and he loved to joke. He was just great fun to be around. As it turned out, I was going to be around him a lot—like for fifty years after that. For the record, Satchel was blazing in Wichita, winning all four of his games and striking out sixty batters, which I hear is still the tournament record. I was lucky enough to see him beat the Duncan boys 5–2, striking out fourteen along the way. That seemed like a routine game for him.

I got another glimpse of my future at that NBC tournament. The organizers had arranged for the winner to play an exhibition game against the Kansas City Monarchs. Satchel lost a close one, but then his opposing pitcher was Bullet Joe Rogan. They must have struck out twelve batters apiece.

The Tigers took away twenty-five dollars each from the tournament, and they all gave me the money to hold so that we could finally buy our car back and return to the palm trees. Unfortunately, the night after the big game, the Monarchs, who were paid to play, and the Bismarck team, which had just won seven thousand dollars, decided to party, and Marcelle, Riggins, and Carr wanted to go out on the town with their old friends.

So around ten o'clock that night, I heard a loud knock on my door. "Hey, Foots!" Ollie Marcelle was shouting. "Open it up, quick." I let him in, and he said, "Give me my cut."

"But you told me not to," I told him. "How are we going to get home if you're spending all your money?"

He stuck out his hand and demanded, "Give me my money!" I didn't see any point in arguing with a guy who lost his temper as easily as Ollie did. But then, about fifteen minutes later, there was another knock on my door. This time it was Bill Riggins shouting, "Foots! Open up. I want my dough." No sooner had I given Riggins his cut than I heard another knock. Before the night was over, almost everybody had shot their wad but me.

The next morning, when I woke up, I could feel the chill in the air. It was early October, and for a southern boy like me, autumn in Kansas wasn't too appealing. Wouldn't you know it? Wayne had one more game lined up for us, in Goodland, Kansas, over by the Colorado border, and his friend with the car was willing to drive us there. Maybe, just maybe, we'd get enough money to buy us our own set of wheels.

Well, we pulled into Goodland on a Saturday morning in the middle of a snowstorm. Our game was canceled, and now we were really busted. We all just stood there on the sidewalk in our uniforms, watching the snow come down, wondering what to do next. All of us, that is, except for Ollie Marcelle. He was still in the back of the car, refusing to get out. "I'm not leavin' this car!" he shouted. And he didn't. The man just drove off with Ollie in the back, and that's the last we saw of the Ghost, who quit baseball and worked as a laborer in Denver for the rest of his life.

We still had to get home. We spent the night in a hobo jungle near the railroad terminal in Goodland, waiting for the next train back to Wichita. Hobo etiquette was to leave pots and pans hanging on trees so that the next poor unfortunate soul could use them, so we picked some corn from a nearby field and started boiling it in one of those pots. Suddenly, a railroad cop appeared at our camp.

"Your father own a railroad, boy?" the man asked me.

"No, sir," I replied.

"Then you got no business being here." And with that he pulled out his gun and shot the pot we were cooking the corn in. We tore out of there so fast, we were out of sight before the water in the pot hit the ground. He took a few shots over our heads as we were running, too, just to make sure we were really going. We caught that freight a few miles down the track, on the other side of town. Goodland? Good riddance!

When we got to Wichita, I called home and told my father what had happened. I told him that Doby Major, my friend from Sarasota, and I wanted to come home, and he said, "Okay, Jay, I'll take care of it." So my father went to see Doby's parents, and they sent us two train tickets. We thought they were going to send us a little money, too, but they didn't. We got on the train with seventy-five cents between us and three days of traveling ahead of us.

In Chattanooga, we bought some day-old bread from a bakery, and that's all we had to eat from Wichita to

Sarasota. Watching the scenery go by, I tried not to think about my stomach even though it was yelling, "Hey, Jay, remember me?"

The worst part was coming into Jacksonville. I knew I was going to run into some of the Red Caps I used to play ball against, and I didn't want to look like a bum. I had this suit with me, so I took it out, folded it carefully, put it under my seat, then sat down on it to press it. Before we pulled into Jacksonville, I went into the rest room, cleaned myself up as best I could, and put on that suit. Sure enough, my old friends recognized me.

"Hey, Foots! You're lookin' good. Where ya been?"

"Man, we've been all over the country," I told them in a voice loud enough to drown out the growling in my stomach.

"How'd ya do?" they asked.

"We did all right," I said, basking in the limelight. "We won some ballgames. Had a good time with Satchel Paige out in Kansas."

While we were laughing and shooting the breeze, Doby kept nudging me, whispering, "Ask them for some money!" But I was too proud. Our day-old bread was two days gone, but we stayed hungry until we got home.

When the train pulled into Sarasota, I felt like I had been gone for years, though it had only been six months. And when I got home, I ate so much my Mama cried.

I slept for two straight days, and when I woke up, I said, "Mama, that's all. I'm not going anywhere ever again." By the look on her face, I could see that a huge weight had been lifted off her. All she said was, "Jay, you can stay right here."

Chapter 4

People Tell Me I Look Good in a Dress

Depending on how he gripped the ball and how hard he threw it, Satchel Paige had pitches that included the bat-dodger, the two-hump blooper, the four-day creeper, the dipsy-do, the Little Tom, the Long Tom, the bee ball, the wobbly ball, the hurry-up ball and the nothin' ball.

The thing about the game, though is not how you hold on to that baseball but how that baseball holds on to *you*. You know what I'm saying now, don't you? You play it as a child, and no matter how old you get, you're still a child when you're chattering in the infield or getting your uniform dirty or taking that lead off first. No matter how much money you make from baseball, I do believe most professional ballplayers would have played it for free—heck, I lost automobiles and got shot at playing those first few years. Just being around baseball is an elixir.

Nowadays, whenever us Negro-leaguers put on the old uniforms for autograph-signings and such, you can just *see* the years peel away. I've seen men lose fifty years in just a few hours. Baseball *is* better than sex. It *is* better than music, although I do believe jazz comes in a close second. It *does* fill you up.

I'm telling you this so you and Mama will know why I had to break my promise to her. I couldn't stay away from baseball, not after I saw Jimmie Foxx take batting practice for the Boston Red Sox in Sarasota a few months after I came home, not after I got a letter postmarked Shreveport, Louisiana.

The letter was from Winfield Welch, who was the chief bellman at the biggest hotel in Shreveport and also the manager of the Shreveport Acme Giants, and he was inviting me to join his ballclub. I showed the letter to my father without saying a word, and he said, "I know you're ready to go, Jay. Go ahead. You might get a chance to catch on with one of those league teams."

We talked to Mama, and while I was prepared for a real fight, she turned out to be pretty easy. She was a wonderful woman. I told you she could sing, but around that time she started getting hoarse. We just thought she had lost her voice, that's all, but it turned out she had a growth inside her throat. Anyway, she gave me her blessing that spring after we told her that the Acme Giants were like a farm team to the Kansas City Monarchs, which they were.

So in the spring of '36 I hooked up with Welch and his players in Monroe. The Crawfords were also there, and they had Satchel back, which gave them five future Hall-of-Famers: Paige, Gibson, Bell, Johnson, and Charleston. We actually played the Craws in some exhibition games, but it was like little leaguers versus major leaguers. They were much better than us, but they also had the advantage of having played winter ball.

That was the first time I faced my future friend. He was a pure flame-thrower back then—someone once clocked his fastball at 106 miles per hour. I couldn't tell you if he was throwing the bee ball or the hurry-up ball because it went so fast I couldn't see it.

The Acme Giants were mostly a traveling team. After we played around Shreveport in the spring, Welch took us up North to play, and we ended up pitching camp in Dunseith, North Dakota, up near the Canadian border. We played in some pretty small farm towns in the Dakotas, Montana, Iowa, and Canada, but even though there weren't any black towns up there, we had no problems getting served in restaurants and hotels. And this goes along with something I've always thought, that wherever I went where there weren't many blacks, things were easier for us than where there were a lot.

You'd think it might be just the opposite, but it was some kind of compensation or something. When there were just a few or no blacks in a town, we were treated better than we were in places like Kansas City or Omaha, because people hadn't formed any opinions, positive or negative, about us. They didn't have all these Jim Crow rules because the issue hardly ever came up.

Here's how royally we were treated in Dunseith: Instead of our looking around for someplace to stay, the town fathers gave us this big house of our own to live in, and we had a ball there. We did our own cooking and everything, and the best thing was that we had a nice big bathtub with hot running water to soak in. That was no common thing back then.

Anyway, at the end of that season, some of us joined up with a team from Mineola, Texas, called the Black Spiders—not the Black Spudders—to form an all-star team that would play in Mexico. We did okay—so well, in fact, that the Mexicans decided to take us into their league. There was one condition, though: We had to beat one of their teams in an exhibition game. But if we did that, we would be spending the winter in Mexico City with the señoritas and the tequila, and that sounded like a good deal.

Only trouble was, we lost. And because we lost, the Mexicans told us to leave their country altogether. You know it's a tough league when they *deport* you for losing.

They dropped us off at the border in Laredo, and because we had nobody there to pick us up, we had to hobo our way back to Shreveport. This time I was too ashamed to call my parents, so I spent the winter in Shreveport with a pitcher named John Markham, who had played with the Monarchs. Through him, I met some of the other Monarchs who lived around there, guys like Bill Simms, Willard "Home Run" Brown, and Eldridge "Head" Mayweather—they called him Head for the same reason they called me Foots. They filled me with stories of the Monarchs, while Winfield Welch filled my pockets with some of the spare change he got as a bellman. What really kept me going was the knowledge that the Monarchs would be in Shreveport that spring, and maybe the owner or the manager would see me play.

Actually, they didn't have to tell me too much about the Monarchs. Along with Rube Foster and Oscar Charleston, reading about the Monarchs in the black newspapers was my main pastime. A lot of people were surprised to find out that the Monarchs' owner, James Leslie Wilkinson, was a white man, but I remembered seeing in the *Chicago Defender* a picture of the Monarchs and the Hilldale Club of Darby, Pennsylvania, lined up on the field before the 1924 Negro World Series, and seeing Mr. Wilkinson—who was called J.L. or Wilkie—standing there with them. From what people would tell me about him, once you got to know Mr. Wilkinson, you didn't even think twice about what color he was. You only knew he was a genius. And he was the most unprejudiced man you would ever get to know.

In terms of Negro league history, Mr. Wilkinson took black baseball into new territory. The Midwest was his home field, so to speak, and he not only had the Monarchs but also promoted the famous House of David, the team from the religious colony in Benton Harbor, Michigan, whose players wore long beards. Over time, there would be a lot of House of David teams, including the Colored House of David, whom Satchel Paige pitched for for a while, wearing a fake red beard. Come to think of it, there weren't many teams Satchel *didn't* pitch for.

Obviously Mr. Wilkinson had a lot of power, and he got even more after he came up with the idea of a portable lighting system for night games. I do believe that if it wasn't for those lights, Negro baseball wouldn't have survived the Depression. Those lights were so popular that other teams would rent them from Wilkie when the Monarchs weren't playing.

Now, they had played night games under the lights as early as 1880, but no professional team had ever done it on a regular basis. What Wilkie did was mortgage his house to buy, for $100,000, a portable system he could fold up, put on six trucks, and erect wherever the Monarchs stopped. The lighting wasn't very good, not by today's standards, and the gas engines that ran it made a heck of a racket—one time, a zoo near where the Monarchs were playing sent someone over to say the animals couldn't sleep because of all the noise. But Wilkie correctly figured that nighttime was the best time for working people to see games. And, again, it wasn't until 1935 that the major leagues made the same discovery.

Sooner than I ever expected, my wish to be noticed by the Monarchs came true. I tore the cover off the ball and didn't miss too many chances at first base. Mr. Wilkinson himself saw me and told Winfield Welch that I was too good to be playing in Shreveport. But Welch told Wilkie that I was his star player, and since Wilkie didn't want to jeopardize his relationship with Welch, he backed off.

But J.L. had an idea for me. A new Negro league, the

Negro American League, was about to start up in 1937, and the Memphis Red Sox and the Monarchs were going to be rivals in the league. So he talked to the manager of the Red Sox, and they bought me from the Acme Giants. Wilkie's plan was to get me into the league until he could find a spot for me on the Monarchs, and he had the power to get other teams to do him favors like that. Wilkie even offered to pay my salary while I was in Memphis, but the owners there liked me and said they would pay it. Winfield Welch never did know how I came to be picked up by the Red Sox. He just thought they had scouted me and liked me.

The Red Sox were owned by a couple of brothers—a doctor and a dentist—the Martins. J. B. Martin was quite an entrepreneur, the owner of a drugstore, a funeral home, and the hotel next door to the ballpark that he built. They paid me ninety dollars a month, no matter the crowds, which was quite a step up from the thirty or so a month I got playing percentage ball with the Acme Giants. And the Red Sox were a pretty good team. Nat Rogers, who once played against Joe Jackson and the banned Black Sox, was a good hitter. Larry Brown was a great defensive catcher who once threw Ty Cobb out stealing five straight times in Cuba and caught *134* games for the New York Lincoln Giants in 1930. The club used me at shortstop and third base a little, but pretty soon I settled in at first.

About halfway through the season, we were in Chicago when I ran into Charlie Henry, who once played for the Harrisburg Giants and now was a promoter in Kentucky who ran the Zulu Cannibal Giants, a team whose players painted their faces, put rings in their noses, and played in straw dresses. They looked like extras in a Tarzan movie, and Charlie gave them these phony African names, like Bebop and Sheba and Limpopo. The Cannibal Giants were so popular that the Miami Giants, my old team, changed their name to the Ethiopian Clowns and started putting on costumes after I left. In the early fifties, when they were the Indianapolis Clowns, Hank Aaron started his career playing with them. Funny thing is, there is a picture of the Ethiopian Clowns with my name on it because somebody mistakenly thought I was the tall guy in the middle. People tell me I look good in a dress, even though that's not really me.

Looking back on it, the idea of playing with the Cannibal Giants was very demeaning. But when Charlie Henry asked me how much I was making and I said ninety dollars a month, he said, "Foots, why don't you come play with us? We're going to Canada and you can make yourself much more money than that."

Back in those days, players jumping around from team to team like this was nothing unusual. We never had any written contracts, only handshake agreements. The contracts only came in after Jackie Robinson went to the majors and the owners tried to protect their players from being taken by white teams with no compensation, like Jackie was from the Monarchs. But before that, the owners practically showed us the way about every man being for himself, because they used to raid each other's teams all the time. That kind of thing was a way of life in the Negro leagues, although later on we began to take team loyalty as a serious business. Most of us, anyway.

So, just like that, I was playing in a grass skirt. I hardly gave it a thought at the time, since this was show business as much as baseball. Again, later on, we wanted our game to stand on its professionalism. The world changed and black people didn't want to be thought of as Zulus or clowns and wouldn't stand for it. But we understood that to draw fans, we were entertainers as well as baseball players, and the game was only part of putting on an exhibition.

Me, I was mostly a straight player all along. I left the clowning to some of the other players on the Zulus. But I did have to wear the war paint and the skirt. Now, you might think a first baseman in a skirt would be especially vulnerable, on line drives and short hops, for example. But the truth was, we had trunks on underneath. Sliding pads, too. See, the skirt came below your knees, so the only exposed part was your shins. Maybe you'd get a little cut up, but what we did was, we slid on our hips, keeping our legs up in the air a little bit. Actually, the whole thing made you feel pretty silly at first, but when you saw that everybody was wearing a skirt, you felt all right about it.

The Zulus might have taken away a little of my dignity, but even in that kind of setting, a tradition was being handed down. The tradition was shadow ball, which the Zulus used to play before the game to warm up the crowd. Shadow ball went way back in our game, and the guys who could do it best were looked up to. I saw the best of all time in Goose Tatum, who was on the Zulus when I was there. You may know his name from the Harlem Globetrotters, but Goose played baseball just as well as he did basketball, and he was just as funny in each. Goose was an outstanding comedian, a great entertainer.

How shadow ball worked was, you'd be taking infield practice with a guy batting out grounders, and you'd be throwing the ball around to the bases and all. And after a while the catcher would hold the ball and pretend to toss it to the guy hitting the ball, who'd hit an imaginary ball. And the fielders would go through this whole routine where they'd make like they were throwing it around. They'd be doing all kinds of tricks until people realized what they were doing—and it would take a while, because they were so good at it.

Goose Tatum would be sitting on first base reading a paper, and they'd "throw the ball" to him, and somebody'd say, "Goose!" He'd nonchalantly reach his hand up, catch it, keep on reading the paper, and throw it on home. Really, you had to see it, because it was very funny the way they did it.

As I mentioned before, the Zulus gave me my name. Syd Pollock, who was handling the publicity for Charlie Henry, remembered me from the Miami Giants, but he got me confused with Buck O'Neal, the bootlegger who owned the team. So my name went up on the placards as Buck O'Neil, and it's been that way ever since, although the black papers didn't get around to calling me that for a while.

Us Cannibals were based in Louisville, and when we returned we had a game with my old ballclub, the Memphis Red Sox. Dr. Martin told Goose Curry, the Red Sox manager, "Don't come back to Memphis unless you bring O'Neil." So Goose offered me a raise, up ten dollars from the ninety dollars a month I was making with them before, and I played for the Sox for the last month of the season.

As it turned out, after four years of scuffling in three different countries, after being shot at and deported, after sneaking out of boarding houses and onto freight trains, I was finally in the right place at the right time. Two events made that possible. First, the first baseman for the Monarchs, Head Mayweather, broke his leg, and then Dr. Martin brought in Double Duty Radcliffe from the Cincinnati Tigers to manage the Red Sox. Double Duty had his own first baseman, Jelly Taylor, whom he brought in. So now I was free to go, and Kansas City wanted me.

I knew I was going to the heart of America. I didn't know I was going to the center of the universe.

Chapter 5

18th and Vine

Imagine what it would be like playing for the New York Yankees in the 1950s, alongside Mickey Mantle and Yogi Berra and Billy Martin. Then imagine what it would it be like staying in a fine New York City hotel, like the Waldorf-Astoria, and coming down every morning to breakfast, nodding hello to Frank Sinatra or Doris Day or Fred Astaire as you pass by their tables.

Well, that's what it felt like for me, playing for the Kansas City Monarchs in the late thirties and early forties, staying in the Streets Hotel at 18th and Paseo, and coming down to the dining room where Cab Calloway and Billie Holiday and Bojangles Robinson often ate. 'Course, some of them were having supper while we were having breakfast, and vice versa. "Good morning, Count," I'd say. "Good evening, Buck," Mr. Basie would say. As somebody once put it, "People are afraid to go to sleep in Kansas City because they might miss something."

Nowadays that downtown neighborhood is kind of sleepy, although we have some plans to wake up the ghosts. But we could never bring it back to its glory days. At 18th and Vine, you couldn't toss a baseball without hitting a musician, and you couldn't whistle a tune without having a ballplayer join in. Baseball and jazz, two of the best inventions known to man, walked hand in hand along Vine Street. We had Satchel Paige and Satchmo Armstrong; Blues Stadium, where we played our ball, and the Blue Room at the Streets, where we had a ball.

New Orleans might have been the birthplace of jazz, but Kansas City is where it grew up. And the same goes for Negro league baseball, which started on the East Coast but came of age in KC. In fact, it was right around the corner from 18th and Vine, at the Paseo YMCA, where Rube Foster and some of the other owners of black baseball teams, as well as a few influential sportswriters, met on February 20, 1920, to organize the Negro National League. Their motto was, "We are the ship, all else the sea," and sure enough, they set sail from Kansas City that day.

There's a good history of the Negro leagues by Robert Peterson called *Only the Ball Was White,* but that title is not strictly true, considering that J. L. Wilkinson was also white. At first. Rube Foster didn't want him to own a club in the Negro National League, figuring the organization should be exclusively Negro, but Wilkie was a respected man in both the white and black communities in Kansas City, and besides, Foster needed Kansas City, and Wilkie held the lease to the ballpark. The other owners prevailed upon Rube to change his mind.

The son of a college president, Wilkie played a little cornfield ball in Iowa, until the manager of his semi-pro team took off with all the money. Right then and there his teammates decided Wilkie would be a better manager than a pitcher. He went on to organize the All Nations, a barnstorming mixed-race and mixed-gender team—his second baseman was a woman named Carrie Nation—that traveled along with an orchestra and a wrestling team. (Jose Mendez, the great Cuban pitcher, played for the All Nations in the field and in the orchestra, on cornet.) The All Nations started out in Des Moines, but after a while, they operated out of Kansas City, and that's how Wilkie came to be so well known in the black community.

Wilkie borrowed some of the best players from the All Nations—Mendez, Plunk Drake, Frank Blukoi, and John Donaldson. Let me tell you about Drake and Donaldson. Plunk, when he and Satchel Paige were pitching for the Birmingham Black Barons in '27 or so, taught Satchel how to throw "the hesitation pitch," where Satchel would kick his front leg up so high it eclipsed the sun, hold it for a split second, and, just when the batter was wondering when he was going to throw the ball, throw it. That would have batters all tied up in knots trying to hold back on their swing.

Well, John Donaldson also influenced Satchel. He was the first guy to go barnstorming his way up and down the Dakotas, pitching for whatever team would pay him. He showed Satchel the way, and the fact is, there are many people who saw them both who say John Donaldson was just as good as Satchel. He was a fantastic left-hander who once pitched three no-hitters in a row, and he was throwing a slider—a hard curve, as hard as a fastball—before anyone knew you could throw a hard curve. They say John McGraw said he'd give fifty thousand dollars for Donaldson if he'd been white. *If he'd been white!* We heard that a lot about a lot of our players through the years.

Well, anyway, Wilkie put them on his new Kansas City team. At first they were called the Browns, but Donaldson suggested they call themselves the Monarchs after an earlier team in Kansas City. Like I said, Wilkie moved in both black and white worlds, and a Kansas City native name of Casey Stengel told him about some good young ballplayers he had seen playing on the 25th Infantry team at Fort Huachuca, Arizona. And that's how solid men like Bullet Joe Rogan, Dobie Moore, Heavy Johnson, Lemuel Hawkins, and Bob Fagan came to the Monarchs.

You know already that I believe Bullet Joe belongs in the Hall of Fame. He was a big, smooth, strong man, Bullet Joe was, and he could do it all. He would pitch a game one day, play in center field the next, and he would hit cleanup. I do believe there has never been a better fielding pitcher anywhere, anytime. In fact, the other day I got to thinking about fellows like Bullet Joe and Leon Day, and I realized something: Go back and look at all the black pitchers in baseball. Guys like Bob Gibson and Vida Blue, they were all pretty good athletes, could run and hit and field and throw. Whereas some of the white pitchers I knew couldn't have played anything else but pitcher. They had that great arm, but other than that, they wouldn't have made it at another position.

J. L. Wilkinson himself had a good eye for talent. In 1922, he plucked second baseman Newt Allen from the sandlots of Kansas City. When I got there, Newt was in his mid-thirties, but even after sixteen years he was an excellent second baseman, and he had six more good years left in him. He could make all the plays around the bag, and I've never seen a second baseman with as good an arm. He was a second-place hitter who could bunt, drag bunt, hit behind the runner. We called him the Colt, but the Cubans called him the Black Diamond after he played down in Havana one winter. Newt liked the name so much that when he got back home he had a dentist cap one of his front teeth in gold and put a diamond in it.

I believe the greatest compliment ever paid Newt was by Frank Duncan, his old buddy from Lincoln High and one of our catchers. "I have watched Newt play for over twenty years," Frank once said, "and I still get a thrill when I know he's going to put on that uniform."

Speaking of Frank Duncan, he got to Kansas City when Wilkie traded three players and a thousand dollars that same year, 1922, to Rube Foster's Chicago American Giants to get Newt's old buddy back together with him. Frank was with the Monarchs for around twenty-five years. He was an excellent defensive catcher and was later one of the very best managers in all Negro ball.

Some of the other teams in the Negro National League might have been floundering, but Wilkie was building himself a juggernaut. Another league, the

Eastern Colored League, was formed in 1922, so Rube had to watch his back and his front. He and Ed Bolden, who ran the ECL and owned the Hilldale Club of Darby, Pennsylvania, came to a truce in the summer of 1924 and agreed to play the first Negro World Series that fall. The Monarchs finished 55–22 that season to beat out Rube's Giants and earn the right to meet Hilldale in a best-of-nine series that was spread among Philadelphia, Baltimore, Kansas City, and Chicago, so that more black people could see the event.

It was Wilkie's boys, most of whom he had found himself, against Bolden's mercenaries, like Louis Santop, Biz Mackey, and Judy Johnson. Keep in mind that Judy Johnson is a Hall-of-Famer. He was a tremendous-hitting third baseman who played for something like twenty years. And the other two may as well have been in the Hall. Santop, who was called Top, was black baseball's first big home run hitter, and I believe he was called "the Black Babe Ruth" before Josh Gibson got that title later on. In fact, an exhibition game was set up in Philadelphia one time between Hilldale and the New York Yankees just so that Top and Ruth could go up against each other. And while Top impressed everybody, the Babe got the last laugh with a home run that went clear out of the ballpark to win the game.

And Biz Mackey? He was the man Roy Campanella

said taught him how to catch, when Biz was player-manager later with the Baltimore Elite Giants. Biz may have been the best pure defensive catcher ever, and was also a hell of a hitter.

Bullet Joe Rogan—the Negro leagues' Christy Mathewson—was magnificent in the Series, winning three of the games, one of them with a single in the twelfth inning. And so was Mendez, who was just supposed to be the manager. Mendez once threw so hard they said he killed a teammate with a pitch in batting practice, but by this time he had nothing but guts and guile. His pitching staff was so thin, though, that Mendez had to take to the mound twice. He tied up the series at three games apiece with a seven-hitter before a big crowd at Kansas City's Muehlebach Stadium, and then pitched a three-hit shutout in the ninth and final game in thirty-degree cold in Chicago.

I remember reading about that game down in the eighty-degree weather in Florida. In 1994, when the Kansas City Royals held a special Negro Leagues Night at Kaufman Stadium, they asked me what uniform the Royals should wear that night. I could have chosen the one worn by the '42 Monarchs, the best team I ever played on, or by the '55 Monarchs, the last Monarchs team I managed. But I selected the 1924 Monarchs' uniform. When I looked at Tom Gordon and Brian McRae and Jose Lind in those beautiful white pin-

stripes—just like the Yankees' uniforms—I saw Joe
Rogan and Newt Allen and Jose Mendez. That's one of
the great things about baseball, if you think about it.
Yesterday comes so easy. You look at the guy now
catching for the Yankees, and you might remember
Thurman Munson or Yogi Berra or even Bill Dickey.

The Monarchs were so strong they outlasted the
Negro National League. Wilkie had to drop out of the
league in 1931 because it was dragging the team down,
and the league died the next year. By then, though,
Wilkie had come up with his greatest innovation,
night baseball. He was also the first team owner to
truly take advantage of the bus. Pullman cars might
have been more comfortable, but buses could get his
players to places that didn't have depots, and with no
waiting time. The small towns were sometimes more
lucrative than the big ones because the Monarchs were
a bigger deal to them, and Wilkie could get a better
percentage of the gate. By the time I joined the Monarchs, the bus had two trailers, so the players could
bunk down in towns with no hotels, or at least no
hotels for black folks. And in one of the trailers, we
even had a little kitchen where you could cook if you
needed to.

This was a shrewd man. Even before Branch Rickey
supposedly invented the farm system, Wilkie was us-
ing the All Nations as a minor league team for the

Monarchs, stocking it with players who were either too young or old. He was also big on promotions like beauty pageants and Ladies Day.

But he was also a decent man. When I got to know him, I realized I was in the company of a man without prejudice, the first man I had ever known who was like that. I was from the South, mind you, so I was unaccustomed to meeting a white man who treated me the way he would his own son. If a hotel was short of rooms, Wilkie thought nothing of bunking with the manager or me. He never missed a payroll, which is saying something, and he often gave players advances on their next season's salary. When Eddie Dwight wanted to open an ice cream shop, "Dad"—that's what we called him—arranged for the bank loan himself.

Wilkie had the players over to his house all the time. His wife was a very nice lady who owned an antiques store. His son Dick became a pilot in the Air Force, and after the war, Wilkie bought a plane so that Dick could fly us members of the Satchel Paige All-Stars all around the country.

Getting back to the Monarchs: They were the beacon of black baseball long before I got there. The Great Depression hit them, too, but that made Wilkie even more determined to take the Monarchs to parts unknown. Because Mr. Wilkinson always insisted on gentlemanly behavior and a good suit, the Monarchs created favorable impressions of African-Americans in places that had never seen one before. During the early thirties, the Monarchs were almost strictly a road team, playing a lot of games with the House of David teams, who brought in people like Grover Cleveland Alexander, Babe Didrikson, and Dizzy Dean's father to goose the gate. The one good thing about the Depression is that it brought black and white a little closer together, if only because people were too poor to be picky about the company they were keeping.

The Monarchs didn't get back into league play until 1937, when they joined the new Negro American League, and Kansas City was glad to have them back home. Opening Day that year was such a big deal that two fifty-piece bands marched the team to Muehlebach Field, where more than twelve thousand people gathered. Sure enough, the Monarchs won the pennant that year, beating the Chicago American Giants in four of the five games of their championship series.

They hardly needed a celery stalk like myself. But there I was, John Jordan O'Neil, heading off in the spring of 1938 to play first base for the Kansas City Monarchs. *The Kansas City Monarchs.* It had the same meaning as the New York Yankees would have had for a boy forty years ago. Just to tell the fellas back home, very cool-like, mind you, "Yeah, I'm going to be playing for the Kansas City Monarchs," was quite a thrill. Quite a thrill. *The Kansas City Monarchs.*

Maybe it's because my memory has failed me, or maybe it's because I was trying so hard to be cool that I blocked it out, but I don't remember much about my first game with the Monarchs except that I played right field in the first game of a doubleheader. Head Mayweather was at first base that game, still hobbling on his broken leg. In the second game, I played first. A dozen years later, I was still there.

Being a Monarch didn't hit home until a game during my first week in Kansas City. The inning ended with a routine groundball to second base and a throw over to me for the putout. I trotted off the field thinking, damn, I just took a throw from Newt Allen! I had been reading about Newt Allen ever since I was a kid. He had been a Monarch since 1922, and I had just taken a throw from him. I felt as if I was standing outside myself, watching it all happen, like seeing myself in a movie.

While we're at it, I might as well go around the horn. Ted Strong, who moved to the outfield a little later on, was our shortstop, maybe the tallest shortstop ever to play the game. He was darn near seven feet tall, a switch-hitter with tremendous power—I saw him hit mammoth home runs from both sides of the plate in one game. Ted was like Cal Ripken, only bigger. They put him at short because he had great hands and a rifle arm. In fact, he was one of the first real tall guys who could do a lot of things. Now, of course, tall guys are all slick just like he was, but back then it was a shock. Ted went on to play for the Harlem Globetrotters as one of their captains.

Ted should have played in the majors. He was truly one of the greatest athletes I've ever seen, although, truth be told, he might have been better if he wasn't so easily led astray. Ted was the type of guy who, if I came down and met him in the hotel lobby and said, "Come on, Ted, let's go to church," he'd want to go. But somebody could beat me down there and say, "Let's go to this dive down the street and drink all night," and he'd be all for it. That was Ted—he'd blow either way. There was the time Ted, Satchel, and Willard Brown disappeared during the 1946 Negro World Series, but I'll tell you about that at the right time.

Our third basemen were Indian Joe Cox, who was so light-skinned he could pass for white (and buy food for us), Packinghouse Adams, and Rainey Bibbs, who joined us in midseason. Like Ted Strong, Rainey was something of a two-sport star, too, having played college football in Indiana. The veteran Frank Duncan was our best catcher. Frank could be mean on the field, but he was sweet off it. And he was testimony to the close relationship between baseball and jazz—

Frank was married to Julia Lee, who was Harry Truman's favorite blues singer. I believe she even performed at the White House.

In the outfield, we had two fast guys, Bill Simms and Henry "Streak" Milton, and two of the strongest men I've ever played with, Turkey Stearns and Willard Brown. I've already told you a little bit about Turkey, who was so crazy about hitting he talked to his bats like they were his children. Willard Brown was something else, too. He had almost as many nicknames as I did: Home Run, Sonny, Willie, and, most often, *Eso Hombre*—that means "That Man" in Spanish, and it came from when he played in Latin America and hit so many tape-measure homers that the folks down there used to say when he came up, "Here comes that man again."

Some people just called Willard lazy. You would think he was loafing, and you always felt he could have done a little more than he did. He'd hit the ball out of the park so easily you'd think, hell, he could have hit it farther if he wanted to. But I think he was such a natural athlete that he made everything look easy.

When I say Willard was a calm man, I mean it. He used to carry around *Reader's Digest* in his hip pocket to give him something to do out in center field. But, man, he could hit, although he wasn't what you call selective—he once hit a home run on a ball that had bounced in the dirt. When the color barrier was lifted in 1947, Willard got a call from the St. Louis Browns, and although he is credited with the first American League home run by a black player, he was released after only twenty-one games in the majors. I'll tell you more about that later, but I'll tell you now that I was happy to take him back when I managed the club.

The strength of the Monarchs, as always, was the pitching. One sportswriter wrote that our infield should be arrested for vagrancy since we spent most of our time standing around doing nothing. The ace of the staff was my great, good friend Hilton Smith, who had marvelous control, a live fastball, and one of the best curveballs I have ever seen. He also had the guts of the devil. A lot of people don't know about Hilton, because he pitched in the shadow of Satchel Paige in the forties. But Hilton was an outstanding pitcher long before Satchel came to the Monarchs.

I know that late in Hilton's life he was kind of bitter about being in Satchel's shadow, the fact that Satchel would pitch the first three innings many times and Hilton would come in and pitch the last six, yet Satchel would get all the newspaper headlines. But listen, I was Hilton's roommate for ten years, and I can tell you Hilton never brooded about it then. He was playing for a salary, just like everybody else, and this was his job. Satchel was pitching in a ballgame just about every night to draw a crowd, and someone had to pick him up. Hilton Smith wasn't the only man pitching behind Satchel Paige; everybody who pitched did that.

'Course, now, I'm not saying Hilton didn't ever *think* about it. Hilton's arm was kind of crooked, kind of bent up a little, while Satchel's was long and straight. Somebody asked him once, "Hey, why is Satchel's arm so straight and yours is crooked like that?" And Hilton said, "I'll tell you why. Satchel pitched three—I pitched six!"

In our leagues, they knew all about Hilton, believe me. He pitched a perfect game against our arch rivals, the Chicago American Giants, the year I came to the Monarchs. Over a six-year period, he was 129–28. Hilton was also a great hitter. Like Bullet Joe Rogan, he'd pitch one game and then go to play the outfield the next. A graduate of Prairie View A&M, Hilton was the son of a teacher. He was a quiet man, and we got along splendidly. When he died in 1983, we were both scouting for the Chicago Cubs, and I still miss him.

As for the other pitchers, we had Red Bradley, who had an outstanding fastball; Floyd Kranson, who was fair-skinned and a pretty fair pitcher; Johnny Markham, who threw a knuckler; a hard-throwing kid named Randolph Bowe; and our manager, Andy Coo-

per. Lefty, as we called Andy, didn't pitch much; he
was in his forties and long past his prime, but he did
pitch a no-hitter that season. He was the best manager
I ever played for, and I played for some good ones. He
was also a father figure and a teacher, and he helped
me a great deal, as he did other players who were still
developing. He could be stern if he had to be, but he
was easy to be around. Some managers might say,
"You guys get in by midnight or else!" Andy would
say, "You know our curfew is midnight, and I know
you guys know this. So I know you're gonna be in by
midnight." With Andy, you felt like you were violat-
ing a trust if you broke the rules, so he got better
results than the manager who tried to be tough.

I left out the first baseman. Buck O'Neil—or John or
Johnny O'Neil, because the papers hadn't yet caught
on to Buck—batted sixth most of the year, hit .258
with a little power, and my teammates and the fans
liked my aggressive style and the way I handled myself around the bag. Modesty aside, I could play a
little, and although I was technically a rookie, at
twenty-six I wasn't exactly wet behind the ears. The
Memphis Red Sox were the best team in our league in
1938, which was something of a disappointment since
I had just left them, but other than that, it was a glorious thing to be part of the Monarch family.

And it really was a family. We slept together, ate

together, and after the game, we'd drink and dance together. My first year I roomed at the Streets with Henry Milton, but on the road I usually bunked with Hilton Smith. Milton at home, Hilton on the road.

We were always very aware of our image. There was a tailor on 18th Street named Meyers, whom Wilkie kept on call to make sure everyone had a nice set of clothes. The Monarchs weren't allowed to wear their baseball jackets outside the park. A Monarch never got into a fight on the street. A Monarch never shot craps on the bus or in the hotel.

The Booster Club, which was made up of black merchants, fraternal organizations, church deacons, and most everybody else, also took good care of us. Whenever the Monarchs won a championship, they'd give the players a beautiful gold baseball charm for their watch chains, and when I saw all the ones Newt Allen had, oh, how I envied him.

Another thing I noticed that first year was that some players never stopped being a Monarch, even though they were no longer playing. Two men in particular were very helpful to me. One of them was Newt Joseph, who had been the third baseman for many years before retiring in 1935. He and Newt Allen were roommates and nearly inseparable, which is kind of funny since they were the only two Newts I'd ever heard of before this Gingrich fellow came along. Anyway,

Newt Joseph was a fun-loving guy who actually managed the Monarchs for a while; there's this wonderful
picture of Newt holding a gun on his players to keep
them in line. When I got to know him, he was running
a very successful cab stand downtown. I would hang
around that cab stand for hours, talking baseball with
Newt. In his day, he was a great sign-stealer, and he
taught me some of his tricks. He also gave me scouting
reports on all the players and pitchers in the league,
what to look for from certain pitchers, where to play
certain hitters, which catchers I could steal on. What
he taught me not only helped me a new player to the
league but also as a manager later on.

My other mentor was Wilbur "Bullet Joe" Rogan,
the guy I had first seen at that NBC tournament a few
years before. He had just finished his pitching career
when I arrived and was dividing his time between
umpiring and working in the post office. As good a
pitcher as Rogan was, he was adept at the plate—in
1924 he led the National League in wins and finished
second in batting (.411!). Wilbur taught me a lot about
hitting. I had problems handling pitches on the inside
part of the plate, and it didn't take pitchers long to
figure this out, so I was seeing a lot of balls thrown at
my hands. Wilbur and I would go out to the ballpark
early, and he would throw batting practice to me before anybody else got there. He taught me to stand

back in the batter's box and away from the plate. "The pitchers are going to see you away from the plate," he'd say, "and they're going to throw the ball outside, so you just step into the ball, which is the way you hit best. When the pitchers come back inside, just speed that bat up, swing a little quicker." He also taught me the proper footwork, how to hit off the balls of my feet and not the heels. Needless to say, my hitting improved a lot. Within two years, I was up around .345.

At the Negro Leagues Museum in Kansas City, which is now at 18th and Vine, there's a little video exhibit called "Ask the Coach." I'm the coach. I talk about hitting. But when I talk about hitting, I'm only passing on what Bullet Joe and Newt Joseph taught me. From what they and loads of other people told me, I would say that the most important advice about hitting is to wait for the pitcher's best pitch, because you're going to get his best pitch three out of four times. If you learn to hit his best pitch, you're going to get to him, so it's worth it to wait him out. 'Course, if he realizes that, he may try and change on you, start throwing you something else three out of four, and you have to have sense enough to wake up to that. It's all part of the checklist in your head that you go through when you hit.

There was something else about the Monarchs. Because we played under those lights so much, we really had a home field advantage wherever we were. We knew how to play those lights. For example, the hardest ball to see was the one that would go real high, above the lights, which were no higher than a telephone pole. Well, we knew where those balls would come down. Who says the old-timers didn't play scientific baseball?

One thing the players do nowadays that we didn't was to make big money and drive fancy cars, but I don't think they have what we had, which was each other. I remember there was this young player with the Monarchs from the rural South. He had a wonderful mind, but he couldn't read. He didn't want us to know that, though, so he would come down in the morning, buy the paper, and toss it to one of us and ask, "What did Jimmie Foxx do last night?" One paper was usually good for three or four of us, and this kid would hold open the newspaper and repeat verbatim what he had just heard, who beat whom, who pitched what, how Jimmie Foxx did last night. He looked like he was reading, but he was just repeating.

One day he was "reading" the baseball scores, but he was turned to the wrong page. He was sitting by me, and I saw it. But I didn't want to embarrass him, so that night I took him aside and said, "I know you can't read." He just looked down at his feet and said, "No, I can't." When I asked him if he wanted to learn, his face lit up. We got a primer, and Hilton Smith and I and some of the other guys started working with him, taking turns teaching him at night. He really took to it, and eventually he got his high school diploma.

Some of the other players, and their wives, thought I was in need of help, too. I was single, you see, and pretty old at that for a bachelor, so everybody was trying to fix me up. Seems like every day somebody would come up to me and say, "Buck, I've got somebody I really want you to meet." It was kind of amusing, really. Maybe the wives thought I might be putting bad thoughts in their husbands' heads, but they were just trying to be nice, I guess.

Anyway, I wasn't ready to settle down, not yet anyway, partly because I knew how tough it would be to be married to a ballplayer. Besides, there were worse places in the world to be single than Kansas City. The Booster Club was always sponsoring these beauty contests before games, and they never lacked for attractive women. And though I never was much for what Satchel Paige called "the social ramble," I did love to go out and listen to music.

There must have been fifty night clubs between 12th and 18th Streets: the Hey-Hay Club, the Chocolate Bar, the Lone Star, the Stork Club, and a wild place called Dante's Inferno that featured waitresses in devil costumes, female impersonators, and a half-man, half-woman comedian called Mr. Half-and-Half. These were the wide-open days of Boss Tom Pendergast in Kansas City, and anything went, including prostitution, gambling, and reefer. Some clubs had what they called "spook breakfasts," morning jazz shows for folks who hadn't yet gone to bed or workers who wanted to put a little bounce in their day. Many was the guy who left the bus stop to hear what was going on and never got to work.

The club owners loved the Monarchs to patronize their establishment because we attracted a crowd, so they often gave us free drinks. We all might have become drunks, but most of the bartenders had been instructed by Wilkie to cut us off if they thought we couldn't handle any more. Oh, some of the Monarchs succumbed to temptation, but mostly we tapped our feet to Andy Kirk's Twelve Clouds of Joy, the Blue Devils, the Count Basie Orchestra, the Jay McShann Orchestra, the Bus Moten Orchestra. I heard Charlie Parker and Lester Young and Harry Edison before they became famous. I stayed at the Streets and ate in the same dining room, the Rose Room, with Cab Calloway, Fats Waller, Big Joe Turner, Dinah Washington, Duke Ellington.

I got to be good friends with Count Basie. He was from Red Bank, New Jersey, so he was something of a Yankee fan, and we bet on the Yankee games whenever he was in town. I always bet against the Yankees, which wasn't a good idea in the late thirties and early forties, so Bill Basie walked off with more than a few of my dollars. Another great musician I called a friend was Lionel Hampton. Hamp was a baseball fanatic who loved the Monarchs. When I managed the team in the late forties, we gave him a uniform and let him coach first base. "You're coming to so many games, we might as well put you to work," I told him.

As much as I liked Saturday nights, I think I liked Sundays even better. They held church services an hour earlier when the Monarchs were in town, and the thousands of fans we got—both black and white—were dressed so nicely and seemed so excited that you couldn't help but feel you were part of something special. And not only when you were in Kansas City, either. We carried ourselves like Monarchs wherever we went, and to people all over, we were Monarchs. We were in the front row, man, the front row. We stayed at the best hotels, ate in the best restaurants; they just happened to be black. Every day we frequented the best nightclubs, saw the best entertainers in the world.

I no longer had to worry about my black book of little rooming houses, where you might not get hot water; now, I was staying at the Vincennes Hotel in Chicago, on the South Side, a big, fine hotel where they had the Platinum Lounge. Or the Majestic Hotel in Cleveland, the Dunbar in D.C., the Slaughter in Richmond—great food! And when we'd play up North, in Minnesota and in Canada, we'd even get to stay in integrated hotels. Years before, J. L. Wilkinson's All Nations used to have to sleep on the ballfield; they'd have to pitch tents and sleep in the dirt. By the time I got to the Monarchs, blacks were in a new world. I knew that overall, of course, we weren't yet where we should be. There was still a ways to go, and still is today. But to be a Monarch was a taste of something special, the good life.

A white sportswriter once coined the expression "Oh, to be young and a Yankee." Well, I was young and a Monarch, and, all in all, I didn't think it could get any better than that.

But it did.

Chapter 6

Seems Like I Been Here Before

Everybody knows Satchel Paige. Or, rather, everybody knows *who* he was. But few of us actually knew him, and I count myself one of the lucky ones.

Mention Satchel nowadays, and people will remember that he pitched in the majors when he was fifty-nine, or that he was a colorful showman, or that he had those six rules of living. While all those things are true, they make him out to be more of a clown than a man, and I just want to set the record straight.

Let me start out with a story that shows a part of Satchel that no one ever hears about. One time we were on the road with the Monarchs in Charleston,

South Carolina. When we got to Charleston, the hotel rooms weren't ready yet. So he said, "Nancy"—you remember why he called me that, right?—"Nancy, c'mon with me. We're gonna take a little trip." Well, we went on over to an area near the harbor called Drum Island. That was where they had auctioned off the slaves, and there was a big tree with a plaque on it, marking the site of the old slave market. Satchel and I stood there, silent as could be, for about ten minutes, not saying anything, but thinking a whole bunch of things. Finally, Satchel broke the silence.

"You know what, Nancy?" he said.

"What's that, Satchel?"

"Seems like I been here before."

"Me too, Satchel."

That was Robert Leroy Paige. A little bit deeper than most people thought.

Before I met the man, I was familiar with the legend. He grew up in Mobile on the same streets that would produce Willie Mays and Hank Aaron. The seventh of eleven children, he picked up his nickname while toting bags at the railroad station. Only seven years old, he couldn't carry more than a bag or two at a time, so he devised a system with a pole and some ropes that enabled him to carry three or four bags. The other young porters made fun of him, said he looked like "a walking satchel tree," and that's how he came to be called Satchel. It was such a famous handle that while the rest of us were listed in box scores by our last names, he was just plain "Satchel."

Like Babe Ruth, Paige spent some time in a reform school, the consequence of having been caught stealing some costume jewelry. It was at reform school that he learned to pitch. When he got out, he was six-foot-three and 140 pounds, and he had a fastball the likes of which nobody had ever seen—or could see. Biz Mackey once said that Satchel threw a ball so hard it disappeared before reaching the catcher's glove. Sure seemed that way to me.

I followed his career in the black papers, but it wasn't easy. Satchel jumped around a lot because, as Cool Papa Bell said, "If you showed him money or a car, you could lead him anywhere." He went from the Mobile Tigers to the Chattanooga Black Lookouts to the New Orleans Black Pelicans to the Birmingham Black Barons to the Nashville Elite Giants to the Cleveland Cubs and then to Gus Greenlee's Pittsburgh Crawfords in 1931. Those Crawfords of the early thirties, though they had no official league designation until Gus created the second Negro National League in 1932, were one of the greatest teams ever assembled, black or white: Oscar Charleston, Judy Johnson, Josh Gibson, Cool Papa Bell, Jimmy Crutchfield, Double Duty Radcliffe . . . and of course, Satchel. One year Satchel went 31–4, not counting all those games he pitched for semipro teams. He got some extra money from all that work, but it probably hastened the loss of his bee ball.

He and Greenlee always clashed over money, and in 1935 Satchel jumped a two-year contract he had just signed—actually signed it at his wedding, when Gus threw him and his first wife Janet a big reception at the Crawford Grille—to go to Bismarck, the team he was with when I first ran into him. He was back with the Crawfords in '36, but in the spring of '37 an emissary of the Dominican Republic dictator Rafael Trujillo lured Satchel to Santo Domingo—the capital city which Trujillo had renamed Trujillo City—to play for this team which was being challenged by a squad assembled by a political rival. See, baseball was such a big thing down there that even a dictator would lose face, and maybe his job, if he didn't have the best ballteam.

Well, Trujillo knew he had to have the best, so he went out and gave Satchel something like six thousand dollars to come down for four months of work. This had never been done before by American ballplayers, leaving their own teams in the States to go to another country to play during the regular season. But Satchel liked to be the first to do things, and he went—and took nine other Crawfords with him, including Josh and Cool Papa. Gus was so angry he had them all banned from the Negro leagues for what was supposed to be life. Actually, it seemed like everybody around the league was going down to the Dominican Republic, to the teams in that league—we lost Chet Brewer, who beat Satchel in a game down there with a no-hitter. But obviously it was the Crawfords who were destroyed, and they would never be the same.

In the end, the Trujillo team won the title, with Satchel winning the championship game—and when the players got home, we started hearing all these horror stories about how they had to win or else. Because Trujillo's soldiers would escort them wherever they went, they thought their lives were in danger and that they'd be shot if they lost! Well, they were good stories—Satchel always told a good story—but I was a little, let's say, skeptical. I could understand Satchel being afraid, with all those guns around, but I couldn't believe they would have been given thousands of dollars and then shot. And the tip-off was that Satchel didn't even come back right away; he was still pitching exhibition games down there when everybody else was home. That tells you something, doesn't it?

Those players who couldn't go back to their Negro

league teams that season formed their own team, the Trujillo All-Stars, although when Satchel got back home and joined up it became the Satchel Paige All-Stars. And they were outdrawing Negro league teams, so they knew they'd be taken back by their teams pretty soon. Satchel had Gus Greenlee over a barrel, and when Gus offered him $450 a week to return to the Crawfords, Satchel refused, saying, "I wouldn't throw ice cubes for that kind of money." So Greenlee sold him to the Newark Eagles for five thousand dollars, but Satchel went the other way, to Mexico, and was banned again for life—as you can see, Satchel had many lives—and made more money than he ever had, but he also came down with his first sore arm. Satchel blamed it on the Mexican food, saying his stomach trouble spread through his body and to his wing. If so, that must have been some nasty food, because the doctors told him he would never pitch again.

As long as he had his fastball, people were willing to put up with Satchel's demands, his speeding tickets, his tardiness. But when he pulled up with a sore arm, well, nobody wanted him. Nobody, that is, except J. L. Wilkinson. I'm not sure what Wilkie's motives were in signing Satchel for the 1939 season, but I'd like to think he was paying him back for everything he had done for Negro baseball. I also think Wilkie had it in the back of his mind that Satchel might not be through. In any case, he knew Satchel could make us all a little money just by being Satchel Paige.

That's how the Little Monarchs were born. Actually, they went by several names, like the Traveling Monarchs, or the Travelers. And really, all they were were our B team. But again, inevitably, they became known as the Satchel Paige All-Stars. Wilkie brought back Newt Joseph to manage them, and off they went into the hinterlands. The Little Monarchs were mostly young guys, although Cool Papa Bell, George Giles, and a few of the older players would go out with the team, too. Wilkie sent one other very important person with them: our trainer, Jewbaby Floyd. He was a licensed masseur, Jewbaby was, and his main job was to nurse Satchel's arm back to health. Every morning and night, he rubbed that arm, applied liniments, and wrapped it in hot towels. Satchel would go out and toss lollipops up there for a couple of innings, and the other team was encouraged to swing and miss just to please the crowds.

And the crowds were there. They were drawing good people out in the boondocks, in little parks that held a few thousand, while we were playing in big-league parks in Chicago, New York, and Cleveland. But he was Satchel Paige, and so they were getting as much publicity as we were, and they were our farm team!

Finally, we met up with Satchel at the end of that season when the Monarchs played the Travelers over in Kansas City, Kansas, at a place called Ward Field. And we really beat up on Satchel, driving him out of the game after four innings and winning 11–0. I don't remember what I did that day, but I do remember he wasn't the same Satchel Paige I had known—but couldn't do a thing against—when he threw the ball by me and my Black Spider boys at the Wichita State tournament back in '35. And it wasn't like we were keyed up to beat him or anything. He just didn't have anything on the ball that day.

But, you know, a funny thing happened around that time. White America discovered Satchel Paige, sort of in the same way that Columbus discovered America. We knew he'd been there all along, but most of the country had to "find" him. And in 1941, the *Saturday Evening Post* did a big story on Satchel and his antics, and some people took away from it the image that black ballplayers acted like clowns. But we saw that article a little differently. We just figured, hey, it was written by a white man who wrote about black base-ball the way he saw it, which was more or less a cir-cus. But we knew it was no circus, and we figured that now people would come to see us and that they would find out whether it was a circus or not. It was more important to us that this was the first time a magazine like the *Saturday Evening Post* had ever written about black baseball.

We weren't resentful that Satchel was getting all the publicity, either, because it meant that we were getting publicity, too. And we felt this might open the doors in the major leagues for some of the fellas. We were elated that one of our own had broken through like that. That's why I say we had to be discovered first, and then people could get to know what it was like to play in the Negro leagues—and the fact is, when other publications picked up on Satchel and did features on him, big magazines like *Time* and *Life,* their tone was much more dignified and respectful. *Time* even made a pitch for big-league integration.

If you think it was rough back then for black baseball to be portrayed in a dignified manner, keep in mind that it's now fifty years later, most people who talk to me still want me to explain the Negro leagues like they think it was, not like I know it was. Maybe that'll change a little because of this book. That'd be real nice.

Not that it wasn't a little strange to see Satchel getting all that ink, because the rest of us black folks figured he was washed up! I mean, here we were, the

Big Monarchs, winning pennants in 1939 and 1940, and the Little Monarchs were getting all the attention. I myself didn't do too bad those years, hitting .345 in '40.

But then another funny thing happened. In 1941, the Little Monarchs were playing my old team, the Shreveport Acme Giants, when Satchel went up to Winfield Welch, who was still the Giants' manager, and told him, "Turn your hitters loose."

"What do you mean?" Welch said.

"Turn 'em loose," Satchel said. "I'm feeling good."

Well, old Satchel struck out seventeen that night, and after the game Newt Joseph got on the horn to Wilkie and told him, "Satchel is ready." I don't know if it was Jewbaby's nursing or a few years of rest, but the arm was almost—but not quite—as good as new.

In a way, Satchel was lucky to have played during a time when there were no team doctors and not much was known about what they call sports medicine nowadays. Back then, if you came up with a bum arm, they'd just tell you you couldn't pitch anymore, like they did with Satchel. Today, they'd want to cut on your arm. But the truth is, I don't think Satchel needed much treatment; I think he just had a tired arm from all those thousands of innings he pitched. He just needed time, and he was lucky, too, that Wilkie believed in him. J.L. knew Satchel would make money for him, but he also believed Satch had something left. I'll say he did! Thirty more years' worth!

Fact is, Satchel was a better pitcher, as in *complete* pitcher, when he came back from his arm trouble. What he lost in velocity he made up for in smarts. I believe this is when he perfected his version of the hesitation pitch he'd learned from Plunk Drake. Let me tell you something about that hesitation pitch, because people have the wrong impression about it— and about Satchel's whole way of pitching. For years and years, I've heard people say he never had to throw a breaking ball because he didn't need one because he could get everybody out with his fastball. Listen to me: Satchel had a breaking ball. It wasn't a Hilton Smith curveball, but you had to be sitting on the fastball so his curve didn't have to be that good, because if you weren't sitting on Satchel's fastball you didn't have a chance. He knew how to set up that strikeout pitch with the curve, like all great pitchers do.

Now, Satchel had been so fast that when he came back his fastball was still better than the average guy's fastball. But he had to do some other things. And that's when the hesitation pitch became his changeup. You couldn't read the hesitation pitch, and the changeup is one of the best pitches in baseball. That was proven in the 1995 World Series by Atlanta's Greg Maddux and Tom Glavine. Yes, many times Satchel Paige got by on his changeup!

When Satchel joined us for good in '41, I'm not sure what I expected. But what I found was a kindred spirit. We hit it off right away, two boys from the South, two boys who had seen a lot of road. While he still liked to joke around, I delighted in his serious side. I asked him about his experiences in Cuba and Puerto Rico and Mexico. I talked to him about things nobody else did, and he liked that.

Let me tell you, Satchel was different from what most people made him out to be, including people who knew him. Satchel was part comedian, a fun-type guy, so people never thought of him as somebody who was deep enough to think about, say, wanting to go to Drum Island.

Satchel came from nothing, even less than most black people did back then, and he had a burning desire to prove himself. He did everything he ever aspired to in black baseball, but it hurt him that he could be so popular and still not be on the same level as a white ballplayer. He would often talk to me about whether I thought things would change. And I'd always tell him, "Satchel, it's gonna change one day." And he would say, "Well, Buck, I hope it changes before I get too old to enjoy it." But I guess Satchel didn't want to let people catch him worrying about it, so he'd say things that didn't let you know what he really thought. Once he got himself in a little trouble on the issue of baseball integration by doing that, but hang on a minute or two. I'll get to that promptly.

I'll tell you one thing Satchel didn't like, and that was people making him out to be a black stereotype. Lots of times, the white papers—and the black ones, too—compared him to Stepin Fetchit, you know, that black actor who played in the movies as slow, lazy characters. They'd talk about Satchel's walk, how slow he moved. And yet I knew that the majority of men had to walk fast to keep up with him! He was so graceful, so smooth, you thought he was just ambling along, but, man, you had to hurry up to stay with him. He made those big, beautiful strides. His stride was maybe a stride-and-a-half longer than mine, and I'm six-two. His legs were so long. He didn't kick that front leg up to the sky only because he was fooling around. He *had* to lift it high or it'd get in his way!

Satchel Paige was no Stepin Fetchit. Satchel was not lazy or slow. He could sing, he could dance, he could play the banjo and the ukelele. And if Satchel had ever run into a writer who called him Stepin Fetchit, that man would have had to battle Satchel— and it might have been a pretty good battle, because Satchel had quick hands and he was no pushover.

I will say that later on, when Satchel got to the

major leagues with the Cleveland Indians in 1948, he might have walked slower—because Bill Veeck, the Indians owner, told him to walk slower, to play up that part of him. This is what Veeck wanted, for him to be like a Stepin Fetchit. It wasn't Satchel, but people thought it was, and I guess it made him and Veeck a lot of money, didn't it? And let me tell you, Satchel was never against making money. He'd tell me, "Buck, look at all these big-league parks I'm fillin' up." So what if they just came to see his antics? Satchel knew who he was, and he also knew that by going to the majors and pitching so well at age forty-two as he did, he was opening the door for other black ballplayers.

Well, I guess this chapter has pretty much become all about Satchel, which is fine by me because I was fortunate enough to see him up close. Of course, the stories about Satchel are legendary, and some of them are even true. Like about his fast cars and his wild driving. I know, because I would go out driving with Satchel quite a bit, and Satchel sure had a heavy foot on that accelerator. But he was a good driver. The problem was, Satchel didn't read the maps that much. If he was on a big highway, he was going to stay on that highway. But you've got to get off that road if you're going to get to the ballpark, and Satchel just might ride right on by and not find his way until about the sixth inning. Fact is, that's the reason Satchel would take you with him, because you'd wind up doing most of the driving. He'd put you in charge of finding the right exit.

I also went hunting with him. That was his favorite pastime besides baseball, and Satchel was a terrific hunter. One time we were up in North Dakota and we were staying in a big house where we did our own cooking. Satchel liked to mess around in the kitchen, and he said, "Let's go out and get some prairie chicken and have it for dinner." So we went out, and he was on one fender of the car and I was on the other, with another guy driving, and we got our guns out and got ready to go chase down our kill when we saw it. And along came a big, juicy pheasant cock right across the road. I wanted to shoot it, but Satchel said, "No, no, no—I said we were gonna eat prairie chicken and that's what we're gonna get!" That was Satchel. When Satchel wanted something, he wouldn't settle for something else.

Then, too, Satchel was a conservationist in that he didn't believe in keeping more than one fish or shooting more than one bird. He had a deep respect for every living thing. One time he, I, and Luke Easter, who played with the Grays, were staying at the Sir John Calvert Hotel in Miami after the season, and we decided to go fishing in the Everglades one morning. On the way back from the fishing hole, we passed a mass of water moccasins, squirming and writhing all around the boat. I had never seen so many snakes in one spot, much less poisonous ones. I grabbed a .22 to shoot the snakes, but again Satchel stopped me. "Put that rifle down, Nancy," he said.

"But look at all those water moccasins!"

"Listen," he said, "if these snakes were hanging around the Sir John Calvert Hotel, sure it'd be okay to kill 'em. But this is *their* domain. We're the intruders. Let's just take our three fish and go home."

Cocky as he was, Satchel was given to brooding sometimes. Sunday night after games, we'd all go down to the Municipal Auditorium to dance to the music of Duke Ellington or Lionel Hampton. This one time, Satchel brought his two-month-old baby girl Pamela to the dance. Even at that age, she was a *long* baby, with her head hanging over one end of the pillow and her feet dangling way over the other side. All of a sudden, Satchel said to me, "Nancy, I don't know if this baby is mine or not." And I said, "Satchel, would you look at this child? Do you know anyone else who could have a baby this long?" Then he started laughing.

You know what I was saying about Satchel not reading road maps? Well, Satchel was kind of like that when he pitched. He didn't care much for little details or detours. For example, Satchel never threw at anyone's head intentionally, never threw a spitball or cut a ball, and in the Negro leagues all that kind of stuff was legal. Satchel wanted to prove that he could get you fair and square, by blowing you away or putting one right on the corner.

One time we were in New York playing the Black Yankees, and Neck Stanley was pitching against us. Neck was a cutball artist and he was throwing all these cutballs and we told the umpire, but he just said, "Aw, go on and play." So, to make a point, Satchel went out on the mound with a soda pop bottle top, and he's standing out there cutting up the ball. And Willie Wells, the great shortstop who was playing then with the Black Yankees, saw this and yelled out to him, "Hey, Satchel, are you cuttin' up the ball?" And Satchel said yes. So Willie said, "Well, hell, I'm not gonna play then." See, Willie knew that if Satchel cut the ball, Satchel wouldn't know where it would be going. And with Satchel throwing about ninety-four miles an hour, he could have killed somebody! And guess what, the umpire threw out that ball and told Satchel he couldn't cut any more of them.

By the time Satchel joined up with us, he relied on me to fill him in on some of the hitters in the league—he had pitched to so many guys he could never remember who they were. I had more time and more of an inclination to observe their weaknesses than Satchel did, and I think he realized at that point in his career that he was going to need something more than his fastball.

The way we worked it, Satchel would pitch the first three innings of most games, and then Hilton Smith or Booker McDaniels or Ford Smith would come in and pitch six for the win. That pleased the fans who came out to see Satchel and at the same time saved wear and tear on his arm. Hilton felt he was as good a pitcher as Satchel, but he had to understand that he wasn't the one drawing the crowds. Sometimes Wilkie did the same thing Gus Greenlee did when Satchel was with the Pittsburgh Crawfords, hiring Satchel out to other clubs who needed a gate attraction. Maybe the Memphis Red Sox needed a little attendance boost. Well, Dick Wilkinson would fly Satchel to Memphis for his special guest appearance, the Red Sox would get a full house, Wilkie would get a fee, and Satch would get a percentage of the gate. Everybody made money. I always say that Satchel Paige wasn't just one franchise, he was a whole lot of franchises.

The only trouble with that arrangement was that Satchel got lonely. He made a lot of money, but he missed us Monarchs, he missed the fun. He told Wilkie he was afraid to fly in that plane, but what he was really afraid of was missing something.

We used to kid him about his hitting, and to this

day people think he was a joke at the plate. But in truth he wasn't terrible with the bat. I once saw Satchel hit a ball long enough to be an inside-the-park home run. This was against a team in East Chicago, Indiana. Satch had pitched his three innings, and he was due up in the top of the fourth, so the manager, who happened to be me, had a pinch-hitter all lined up. But Satchel told me, "I can hit this guy." I left him in, and he hit the ball over the centerfielder's head. If it had been anyone else, including someone slow, it would have been an inside-the-park home run. But Satchel was laughing so hard he had to stop at second base to catch his breath. He said, "All right, you can take me out now." Satchel talked about that hit until the day he died.

Another time we were playing a semipro team in Denver made up of guys who worked for the Coors Brewing Company. Satchel was a little wild that day, which was unusual, and he walked two batters. When the next batter hit a little dribbler down the third base line for an infield single, the bases were loaded. One of the Coors players made the mistake, though, of shouting from the dugout, "He's nothing but an over-rated darkie. Let's beat him."

Satchel walked over to me at first and said, "Nancy, did you hear what he said?"

"Yeah, I heard him."

"Well, bring them in."

I thought he meant for me to bring the outfielders in a few steps, so that's what I signaled them to do. "No, Nancy," he said. "Bring them *in*." I brought them in a little more, almost to the back of the infield. "No, Nancy, bring them *all* the way in." So there we were, seven of us, all kneeling around the pitching mound. Satchel struck out the next three batters on nine pitches. The fans gave him a standing ovation, and the guys on the other team apologized for what one of them had said.

For Satchel, making believers out of doubters was sweeter than winning any ballgame. It was as sweet as life itself.

I've got more to tell you about Satchel, but since I told you 1942 was my favorite year, I think I should get a word or two in edgewise about the 1942 Monarchs, who were the best team I ever played with. Someone once asked Newt Joseph who he would take with him if he could play in the major leagues, and Newt replied, "The whole Monarchs team." That's the way I felt about the '42 Monarchs. I do believe we could have given the New York Yankees a run for their money that year.

Frank Duncan was now the manager, having succeeded Andy Cooper, who died rather suddenly in 1941. The new catcher was Joe Greene, who was called Pea because that's what he threw to second base. We got him from the Homestead Grays, where he had to play behind a guy name of Josh Gibson. He had a wonderful pitching staff at his disposal: Satchel Paige and Hilton Smith and Connie Johnson and Cannonball McDaniels and Lefty LaMarque and Jack Matchett. Newt Allen was still around, but the starting second baseman was a good-looking rookie from Dallas, Bonnie Serrell. They called him the Vacuum Cleaner because of his range, and he had a pretty good bat as well, hitting .371 that year. His double-play partner was Jesse Williams, a brash young man who also had tremendous range. Our third basemen were Herb Souell and Newt Allen, and in the outfield we had the familiar faces of Ted Strong, Bill Simms, and Willard Brown, who led the league in both home runs and steals that season.

Me, I hit just .247, but I led the Negro American League in at-bats, with 182, and I made the West team in the East-West game, the Negro leagues' all-star game, for the first time, thanks to the voting of the fans in the black newspapers. The year before, Jelly Taylor of Memphis won the voting among first basemen, but in '42 I beat out Jelly by ninety thousand votes to seventy thousand—although they billed me on the ballot as "Joe O'Neil"—and I guess they figured I was a good choice because I was the only first baseman on the whole West squad. And those nice folks voted me back again two more times, when I was listed as Buck O'Neil.

Let me tell you a little bit about the East-West Game, because for a black ballplayer and black baseball fans, that was something very special. Gus Greenlee began the game in 1933, the same year that the major leagues began their all-star game, and in the same ballpark, Comiskey Park in Chicago. That was the greatest idea Gus ever had, because it made black people feel involved in baseball like they'd never been before. While the big leagues left the choice of players up to the sportswriters, Gus left it up to the fans. After reading about great players in the *Defender* and *Courier* for so many years, they could cut out that ballot in the black papers, send it in, and have a say. That was a pretty important thing for black people to do in those days, to be able to vote, even if it was just for ballplayers, and they sent in thousands and thousands of ballots. It was like an avalanche!

Right away it was clear that our game meant a lot more than the big-league game. Theirs was, and is, more or less an exhibition. But for black folks, the East-West Game was a matter of racial pride. Black people came from all over to Chicago every year— that's why we outdrew the big-league game some years, because we always had fifty thousand people at ours, and almost all of them were black people; not until after Jackie Robinson did any whites come out.

In fact, we kept the game in Chicago because it was in the middle of the country, and people could get there from all over. The Illinois Central Railroad would put on a special coach from New Orleans to Chicago. They would pick up people all through Mississippi and Tennessee, right on into Chicago. The Santa Fe Chief would be picking up people in Wichita and Kansas City. The New York Central would come in from the East.

This was *the* weekend. It was near the last weekend before school started, so a lot of kids would save up their nickels and dimes. In Chicago, all the black stores would sell tickets to the game. I remember in '42 box seats went for $1.65, grandstand seats for $1.10, and it was fifty-cents for a bleacher seat. And those stores on the South Side, from 40th to 50th Streets, like the Ben Franklin Department Store, Monarch Tailors, Harry's Men Shop, the South Center Department Store, they'd all have a big sign out, EAST-WEST TICKETS SOLD HERE. Because that would get people into the store. A guy would come in and buy a ticket, and while he was there he might buy a hat or a pair of shoes.

That weekend was always a party. All the hotels on the South Side were filled. All the big nightclubs were hopping. Lena Horne was at the Regal club, and all the pubs had live entertainment. At the '42 game, Marva Louis, Joe Louis's wife and a wonderful singer, threw out the first ball. If you've seen a heavyweight boxing title fight with all the big shots there, you know what the atmosphere was like for us in Chicago. If you were anybody, you were at the East-West Game. And for many of us, if you were coming to Chicago, you would also be picking up your fall wardrobe.

Only problem was, even though the owners were making out like bandits on the game—the ticket receipts were something like $180,000 over the first eight years of the game—the players weren't getting anything—except for Satchel, of course; he always made his own side deals to take a cut of the gate, which nobody minded because he would help fill up that park. But, you know, we had to get *something,* and that year, 1942, some of us threatened to go on strike and not play the game if we didn't get something. So that's when they started paying each of us a hundred dollars—tipping money for the guys of today, but a lot for us.

There were a couple of significant things that happened at that game, which was played on August 16. Satchel was supposed to start for the West—he'd won a couple of times for the East before—but he showed up late and Hilton Smith started, and he and the New

York Cubans' Dave Barnhill hooked up in a pitcher's duel. After six innings, it was tied 2–2. By then, Satchel had gotten to the park, and Winfield Welch, the West manager, brought him in. But instead of going to the mound, he took a microphone and began talking about what he had told the press a few days before when they asked him about major league integration. Like I told you, Satchel would say things that would be taken wrong, and when he said there might be problems with blacks playing in the South in spring training, and with redneck ballplayers, it seemed as if he was coming out against integration.

Well, that caused quite a fuss, but since Satchel isn't around, maybe I can explain what he was saying. Satchel wanted very much to pitch in the majors. But at that time, in the early forties, our game was reaching its high point. While the big-league game went down when most of its stars went to fight in the war, our game was booming. A lot of us were doing pretty well, and Satchel was the best paid ballplayer in America, making around forty thousand dollars a year.

So I knew where Satchel was coming from. He was torn about the idea of leaving black baseball. Listen, I might rather have played with the Kansas City Monarchs than the New York Yankees if I could have gotten the same money from the Monarchs that I would have with the Yankees. We all had that loyalty to our game.

But the other side of the coin was that if we went to the majors, the whole world would get to see us play. We wanted the whole world to see us play. We wanted to *compete* with the majors. It was great to beat the Homestead Grays, but it would be something else to beat the Yankees or the Boston Red Sox or the St. Louis Cardinals—and that was another thing Satchel said, that maybe it would be better, at least at first, to put a complete black *team* into the majors, not to sprinkle black players around to all the teams.

So anyway, Satchel came into the game and tried to clarify what he said, but to tell you the truth, I didn't hear him because I think he was speaking mainly to the writers. But I do know that when he took the ball, he didn't have his good stuff. He gave up three hits and a run, and when Josh came up with runners on second and third, Satchel walked him intentionally— you didn't want to let Josh Gibson beat you, if you could—and that worked, because the next guy hit into a double play. In the ninth, Satchel again walked Josh intentionally. But this time he gave up a hit to Bill Wright to score two more, and that's what we lost by, 5–2. Of course, I helped to sink Satchel two batters before that when I threw behind Satchel, who was covering first on a grounder to me.

No, this wasn't a good game for me, but these things happen. I went 0 for 4, but I'd like to point out that it took a spectacular play by the great Willie Wells at short to get me out once. I hit it hard up the middle, but Willie went behind second base, speared it, spun around, and threw me out. He could do that and make it look easy.

Although we lost, just being there was a thrill, and I couldn't help but feel proud riding home on the train with Hilton, Satchel, Ted Strong, and Joe Greene. And while I didn't know it at the time, I would be a party to Satchel's making up for his bad performance and then some, just a few weeks later.

We won the Negro American League pennant for the fourth year in a row, but what made this one different was that it got us into the first Negro League World Series since 1927, against the Homestead Grays of the Negro National League. For a fan of black baseball, a Monarchs-Gray World Series was a dream come true, although we were definitely the underdogs. The Grays, who had not only Josh Gibson but Buck Leonard, Sam Bankhead, and Vic Harris, had beaten us all four times we played them that season, although they were all close games. Satchel lost three one-run games to them, so he was hopping mad. And our young guys, Jesse Williams, Bonnie Serrell, and Herb Souell, didn't know enough to be scared.

Jesse was particularly chesty. During batting practice before the first game of the series, at Griffith Stadium in Washington on September 8, he strolled over
to the Grays' dugout like he was the cock of the walk
and started checking out the bats in the rack. He
picked up one that was so chipped it looked like it
was left over from the 1927 Series, and he called out
to Gibson in his squeaky voice, "Hey, Josh, this must
be your bat."

Josh took the cocky youngster aside and said, "Let
me show you something." He pulled a bat out of
the rack that looked brand new except for a spot
the size of a baseball on the fat part of the barrel,
where the finish had been worn clean off. "Son, this
is my bat," he said. "I don't break 'em. I wear 'em
out."

We won the battle of psychological warfare, however. As was his custom, Satchel was playing the gui-
tar and singing in our dugout during their batting
practice. The Grays had a shortstop named Chester
Williams, and he came over to us and said, "Man, you
got nothin' to sing about. Don't you know we're gonna
run you out of the ballpark?"

Satchel just looked at him and said, "Chester, you
see all these people in the ballpark? You know what
Wilkie's gonna do?"

"What?" said Chester.

"Wilkie's gonna give us all the money. He ain't gonna take no percentage out of it."

Well, Chester's eyes just about popped out of his head. No way was Cumberland Posey, the owner of the Grays, going to do that for his team. "That's right," said Satchel, pouring it on. "We made a lot of money for Mr. Wilkinson this year. He's just gonna take out his expenses and give us the rest." Chester flew back to his dugout, and while we went back to our singing, we could see him tell all the Grays what Satchel had just told him, that we were going to get more money than they were, no matter who won the Series. The first pitch hadn't been thrown, and already Satchel had us ahead.

Sure enough, we had their number that first game. I don't know if they were fretting about the money, but their heads were definitely not in the game. Satchel and Josh had been teammates for a long time with the Crawfords and in Puerto Rico, but the greatest pitcher in Negro league history hadn't faced the greatest hitter all that often. Although Satchel had wanted no part of Josh in the East-West Game, in all the Monarchs-Grays games that season Satchel had handled Josh pretty well. And so now all kinds of psychological warfare was going on.

Satchel, of course, was a master at messing with a man's head, especially when he had his good stuff.

And in that first game, which brought in 25,000 people on a Tuesday night, he had it. He set down the first ten Homestead hitters, and with the score 0–0 in the fourth came the big moment of the game. With one out, Sammy Bankhead got a single off Satchel, and then Howard Easterling got another. Now up came Josh.

In that game, Satchel rode Josh mercilessly, telling him as he came to bat each time, "Look at you, you ain't ready to hit. Come on up to the plate. Don't be scared." But Josh also liked to ride Satchel. They liked to kid each other, and it was funny how they'd go back and forth, even though you knew they had the greatest respect for each other.

Satchel had struck Josh out the first time up. But now Josh took that big cut and got it right on the sweet spot of the bat. By the sound of the crack, it was the usual Josh Gibson home run. I can still see that ball streaking across the dark blue sky. But we got a break in that Josh hit it to dead center field, and in Griffith Stadium center field was like the Grand Canyon. The ball went up, up, up—then came down, down, down, and was caught by Willard Brown in front of the wall about 460 feet away.

That ball was hit so long that both runners tagged up and moved over a base. But Josh was out, that was the big thing. And when Satchel got Buck Leonard to end the inning, we all let out a big sigh of relief. Satchel especially, because he didn't give up another hit, and neither did Jack Matchett, who came in to relieve Satchel in the sixth. We broke through on Roy Welmaker late in the game and won it 8–0. I helped out a little with a triple that drove in a couple, but it also helped that we outhit the Grays 13–2 and that they made seven errors! I remember the headline I saw in one paper: JOSH HITLESS, GRAYS MAKE SEVEN ERRORS AS MONARCHS PREVAIL.

After that first game, we played a few exhibition games in little towns as we made our way to Pittsburgh for the second game in Forbes Field. It might seem odd, playing between games of the World Series, but that's the way it was done. World Series or not, there were a lot of folks in those towns who'd pay to see us play. I guess you could say that to folks in those towns, the World Series was seeing their team play the Kansas City Monarchs. But all through those games, we kept thinking of how we'd crushed the mighty Grays and could not wait to get at them again.

When we did, it was a rainy Thursday night, and only about five thousand people were there. But they were to witness the most famous confrontation in the history of black baseball, one that boiled down a hundred years of history into one at-bat. It happened after Hilton Smith was outpitching Roy Partlow and was ahead 2–0. Now Satchel came on to relieve him in the sixth.

"You've been relieving me all season," Satchel told him. "Let me relieve you."

I've been telling about black baseball in lectures and at banquets for a long time now, and more than anything else, this game is what I usually end up talking about the longest. It's the one people ask me to talk about most. So, for those of you who don't know the particulars, I'll set them up one more time—until the next banquet, that is.

In the top of the seventh inning, Jerry Benjamin led off with a triple down the left field line. Satchel looked over at me and said, "Come here, Nancy." And I said to myself, uh-oh, he's got that look in his eyes. I know that look. It's trouble. So I went over to the mound with some trepidation, and he said, "You know what I'm fixin' to do, Nancy? I'm gonna put Vic Harris on base. Then I'm gonna put Howard Easterling on base. And then I'm gonna pitch to Josh."

Now, Satchel might have lived for moments like this, but his teammates sure didn't. This was the World Series! I motioned frantically to Frank Duncan in the dugout. He came to the mound and I said, "Frank, listen to what this fool wants to do." And when he found out, Frank, who knew he couldn't have changed Satchel's mind anyway, just shrugged and said, "Buck, you see all these people out here? They came to see Satchel pitch to Josh." The way he said it, it was like Frank wanted to see that, too. And as Frank walked back to the dugout, I learned right then and there that you don't manage Satchel Paige, you manage the team he happens to be on.

You might be wondering why, if Satchel felt this way, he walked Josh twice at the East-West Game, which more people saw than any of our World Series games. Remember what I told you about Satchel before? That if he had something in his mind, he'd want to do it? Well, I don't think his head was in that place at the East-West Game. It was set on making that speech he gave. Then, too, maybe he felt he didn't have it at the East-West Game, and when the situation came up to walk Josh, it was just the logical thing to do.

But I'll let you in on something. Things had been building between Satchel and Josh since the East-West Game. We were in the team bus late in the season, up in the Blue Mountains east of Pittsburgh, and the bus was stopped while we were putting water in the engine. And Satchel and I were throwing rocks down the mountain when he started talking about when he and Josh were with the Crawfords and they were going through the same mountain and they had this conversation. Satchel said he had told Josh, "You know what they say, that you're the best hitter in the world? Well, I know I'm the best pitcher in the world, and some day we're gonna be on different ballclubs and we're gonna meet up and see who comes out on top." And Satchel said he wanted to settle it once and for all.

So now he and Josh had been getting on each other in the papers about who would get the best of each other in the World Series and all. And with Satchel walking Josh twice intentionally in the East-West Game to load the bases, what better way to settle the argument than by pitching to Josh with the bases loaded? And at that moment, I knew one thing for sure—that Satchel would rather get Josh out in that one at-bat than win the ballgame!

The crowd had figured out what was going on, too, as soon as Satchel threw the first intentional ball to Harris. People had come to expect outrageous things from Satchel, and nobody wanted him to intention-ally walk Josh in the World Series. As Harris trotted down to first, Howard Easterling came to the plate, and as soon as Josh stepped into the on-deck circle, Satchel carried on a conversation with him. "Josh," he called out, "you remember the time with the Craw-fords when we were going over the Blue Mountains?"

"I remember, Satchel."

"Then step on in that batter's box and we'll see who's right."

Man, that place was really buzzing as Easterling loped down to first base to load them up. But Satchel, the great showman, still wasn't through setting the stage. Satchel's stomach problems were famous, and he had some right now. He took off his glove, set it on the mound, and motioned for Jewbaby Floyd. And out came Jewbaby to the mound with a glass foaming over with bicarbonate of soda. Satchel drank it down and let out a great big belch. He was playing the crowd like a fiddle.

Jewbaby walked off the mound and Satchel said, "Okay, Josh, I'm ready." Josh said, "I'm ready, too. Let's get it on!"

I had faith in Satchel, but I must admit I had my doubts, too, because Josh Gibson had no weaknesses as a hitter. So I'm holding my breath as Satchel winds up, throws, and—boom!—a good fastball for strike one. Josh didn't even move his bat.

Satchel says, "Okay, Josh, now I'm gonna throw you another fastball, just about the same place. But it's gonna be a little harder than the last one."

Boom! Strike two. Josh didn't move his bat.

And now Satchel takes off his glove, rubs up the ball, hitches up his pants, and says, "Josh, I got you oh-and-two, and in this league I'm supposed to knock you down. But I'm not gonna throw smoke at yo' yolk—I'm gonna throw a pea at yo' knee."

Boom! Strike three. Josh never even took a swing as the ball smacked into Joe Greene's glove like a clap of thunder.

Josh threw down his bat and stomped back to the dugout. And now Satchel smiled with his whole face and, as we're walking off the field, said to me, "Nancy, you know something? Nobody hits Satchel's fastball."

That was one of the most electrifying moments in thousands of games of black baseball—and I was only ninety feet away! When I told that story to Ken Burns, he liked it so much he ended the Fifth Inning segment of his *Baseball* series with me telling it, which was very nice of him, but I've thought about it since and it was somewhat misleading. What I neglected to mention was that some of the air seemed to go out of Satchel after that. After building to that point, I believe Satchel lost focus on the game a little. And the Grays *did* get to Satchel's fastball after that, to the tune of four runs in the very next inning to cut our lead to 5–4. Fortunately, we scored three more in the eighth and won it 8–4. Again, I helped out a little, getting a hit and a stolen base in five tries.

There's one more thing I have to add about that story. A while ago, someone pointed out to me that in the *Afro-American*'s story about that game, the man wrote that Josh swung at those pitches, that he fouled off the first two and missed the third. Uh-uh. No way.

Josh didn't even swing the bat. Not once. I'm sure of it. I was there. Maybe that writer was there, too, but he must have been watching something else.

After that great win, we weren't about to ease up now, especially with the third game being played at Yankee Stadium. Actually, we played a doubleheader on that day, a Sunday, because thirty thousand fans paid their way in. I told you about those Yankee Stadium crowds—it was just something. That's why we played there, and it was the first time two black baseball teams played a World Series game there. Only the first game counted as a World Series game, and Satchel pitched that one—although maybe he shouldn't have.

Satchel wanted to pitch every game, but he was tired and gave up a couple of runs in the first inning on a Howard Easterling home run into the right field stands. So Frank took him out and brought in Jack Matchett, who shut down the Grays while we came alive. In the third inning, Ted Strong and Willard Brown hit back-to-back homers off Ray Brown, and that opened the floodgates as we won, 9–3. (We also took the second game, 5–0).

By now, Cum Posey was so desperate he brought in Leon Day and some of his teammates from the Newark Eagles for the fourth game a week later at Ruppert Field in Kansas City. Leon pitched a heckuva game and beat Satchel 4–1 (I scored our only run on a hit by

Bonnie Serrell), but the result was disallowed after the Monarchs protested to the league commissioners that Posey had brought in ringers. Cum, who was a brilliant and cagey man, said we had given him permission, but nobody believed that and the game was thrown out.

That left another fourth game to be played, in Philadelphia's Shibe Park. Satchel was scheduled to start, but at game time he was nowhere to be found. We were trailing 5–2 in the fourth when Satchel finally showed up. Seems he had gotten one of his many speeding tickets in Lancaster, Pennsylvania, on his way to Philly. The cops took him to the local barbershop, where the judge was getting his hair cut. When the barber was through, the judge fined Satchel three dollars and sent him on his way to the World Series.

It was a cold, cold night, more like football weather, but nothing could stop us, not cops, not judges, not the weather, not Josh Gibson. Actually, Josh wasn't around too long that night. When Satchel came in, he should have been facing Josh with two on and two out, but instead he was facing Robert Gaston, Josh's backup, after Josh had taken himself out of the game an inning before.

They said later that Josh was ailing, that he was run down and might be real sick. Tragically, we found out that was true a few months later, but during the series we just thought he was having a rare slump, because he wasn't hitting well. Even so, in that second, non-series game at Yankee Stadium, Josh had hit a ball on a line for a triple out there by the monuments in center field. That didn't seem like any sick man.

Satchel shut down the Grays the rest of the way, while we rallied for seven runs, thanks in part to an inside-the-park homer and a triple by yours truly, who had three hits in all. What a thrill! We had swept the Homestead Grays in four straight games and claimed the first true championship of black baseball in fifteen years.

And Satchel was right. Wilkie did give us all the Series money, just like he'd said he would.

Chapter 7

Bring 'Em On

Ken Burns used shadow ball as a metaphor for the Negro leagues. We were the game that was being played alongside major league baseball, but we were lost in the shadow of prejudice—still are lost. We were disorganized, they say. We didn't keep statistics, they say. As Buck Leonard once said, "We were not disorganized, just unrecognized." As for statistics, here's one: Smokey Joe Williams went 41–3 pitching for the New York Lincoln Giants in 1914. Here's another one: Smokey Joe Williams compiled a 20–7 record in exhibitions against major league competition. And another one: Smokey Joe Williams struck out twenty-seven Kansas City Monarchs when he pitched a twelve-inning one-hitter against them in 1930. Smokey hasn't gotten his due in Cooperstown. Not yet, anyway.

Of course, thirty years ago, we received no recognition at all. We didn't have Negro-league scholars like we do now; we didn't have Ken Burns. Do you know who was one of the first people to call attention to the Negro leagues? It was Ted Williams. On the day he was inducted into the Hall of Fame in 1966, he said, "I hope that some day Satchel Paige and Josh Gibson will be voted into the Hall of Fame as symbols of the great Negro-league players who are not here only because they weren't given the chance."

That got the ball rolling as far as the Hall of Fame was concerned. Satchel was the first one to get in, naturally, in 1971, and after him came Gibson and Leonard. In 1973 they inducted Monte Irvin, who was a heckuva ballplayer, but no ballplayer, not even Satchel or Josh, deserved to go in before Rube Foster, for all he did for our game. That first committee had nothing but easterners on it, and they never saw the guys from out West, Smokey Joe Williams and Bullet Joe Rogan and Newt Allen.

People often ask me who was the best this and the best that, and it's hard to decide because there were so many great ballplayers. It's hard even with a Satchel

Paige. Around 1952 a poll was taken by the *Pittsburgh Courier* that asked people who had played in the Negro leagues to select the best Negro league pitcher ever. Hard as it is to believe, Satchel didn't come in first; he lost to Smokey Joe by one vote. Now, to me, Satchel was the best pitcher I ever saw because Satchel got people out easier than anybody I ever saw. But these guys in the poll may have seen Smokey Joe more than they saw Satchel, because they were from the East. Satchel played in the East for a while but spent most of his career playing with the Monarchs.

Yes, we had our geographical biases—and they still exist today. I recently got wind of the fact that Wilmer Fields, who pitched for the Homestead Grays in the mid- and late forties, said not long ago that Ken Burns shouldn't have even had me on his show because I was from the West, and the West didn't have a real Negro league! Now, that was kind of a stupid thing to say. The Negro leagues, after all, were started in the West, by Rube Foster. Some of the guys who played out there are among the greatest players who ever lived. But this just goes to show you what I mean. And this is the reason why the original Negro League Hall of Fame Committee didn't elect anybody from the West other than Satchel. In fact, if I'd been on that panel, the first one I would have voted for would have been Rube Foster, not Satchel.

Having said all that, I feel I have a different perspective to offer. I don't want to hurt anybody's feelings, even if they're in heaven right now, but if I had to choose, here would be my all-time Negro league team:

Catcher: This one is easy. I could have made this pick back in 1938, that time I came down to the field in my jockstrap to see who the man was who was making that sound with his bat. Josh Gibson led the Negro National League that year in homers and batting average (.440), and that wasn't even his best season. Judy Johnson once said that if Josh had played in the majors, "Aaron would be chasing Gibson and not Ruth." Josh was a little rough behind the plate at first, but he got better and better, and he had a rifle for an arm. As happy-go-lucky and innocent as Josh was, though, he had a tragic personal life. I'll get more into that in a bit, because it needs some more space.

First Baseman: We shared the same nickname and the same position, and I only wish I'd had half of his talent. They called Buck Leonard the black Lou Gehrig for a reason, although Buck was a much better fielder. He played for the Homestead Grays for seventeen years, averaging .340 and thirty homers a year, and from 1937 to 1945 he and Josh Gibson led the Grays to nine straight Negro National League pennants. Buck—whose real name was Walter—always

Luella O'Neil, my mother. Although she didn't want to see her little boy leave home to travel around the country and play baseball, she encouraged me to do what I love to do most— play ball.

John Jordan O'Neil, Sr., watching me play ball. My dad told me there was more to life than working in the celery fields, I just had to go out and look for it.

Coach Ox Clemons of Edward Waters College, who not only taught his players the fundamentals of the game of baseball, he taught us about life.

The lovely woman who would soon become my wife, Ora Lee Owens (left, with friend Anne Bird Hickman).

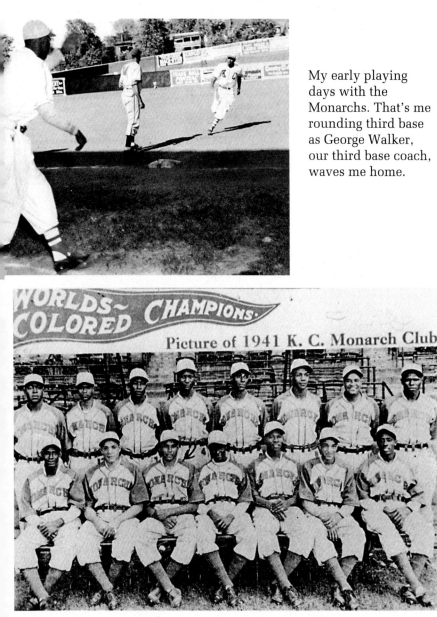

My early playing days with the Monarchs. That's me rounding third base as George Walker, our third base coach, waves me home.

WORLDS~ COLORED CHAMPIONS·
Picture of 1941 K. C. Monarch Club

One of the teams I'm most proud of, the 1941 Kansas City Monarchs. Front row (from left to right): Newt Allen, Rainey Bibbs, Hilton Smith, Jesse Williams, Willard Brown, Allen Bryant, Bill Sims. Back row (from left to right): Joe Reese, Frank Duncan, Jr., George Walker, Connie Johnson, Ted Strong, me, Frank Duncan, Sr., Dick Bradley.

Here I am as manager of the Kansas City Monarchs. Standing alongside me is Dizzy Dismukes, a great friend and mentor. Dizzy taught me a lot about managing a ballclub, lessons I've carried around with me my whole life.

Two of the greatest catchers ever: Josh Gibson (left), the most feared hitter in our league, and Biz Mackey (below), the man who taught Roy Campanella how to catch and the best pure defensive catcher in the game. *(Photographs courtesy of the Negro Leagues Baseball Museum.)*

The best base runner in the league and the fastest man I've ever seen—James "Cool Papa" Bell, enjoying a ball game in the late 1980s with his lovely daughter, Connie Brooks.

The only player to be elected to the Mexican, Cuban, and American Baseball Halls of Fame, Martin Dihigo, *El Maestro.* *(Photograph courtesy of the Negro Leagues Baseball Museum.)*

My good friend Leroy "Satchel" Paige (second from left), checking out some equipment for the season to come. To his right stands Jesse Williams, the Monarchs' regular shortstop, who moved to second base in 1945 to make room for another great shortstop, Jackie Robinson.

Me sitting alongside Monarchs manager Frank Duncan, trainer "Jewbaby" Floyd, and umpire "Bullet Joe" Rogan, the former fireballer.

A night on the town with a couple of friends. That's me with Monarchs owner Ted Rasberry in the middle and "Bullet Joe" Rogan on the right.

Me with Ted "Double Duty" Radcliffe.
"Double Duty" earned that nickname by
pitching the first game of doubleheaders and
catching the second.

A proud moment for
me—in the dugout at
Wrigley Field. In 1962, I
became the first African-
American to coach in
major league baseball.

As a coach, I was usually surrounded by some talented young players. From left to right, there's Lou Brock, Billy Williams, me, and George Altman.

A rare moment off the field: Here I am enjoying a night of jazz with Ernie Banks, his wife, Louise, and singer Joe Williams.

Me (second row, left) and Ernie Banks (second row, third from left) paying a visit to some old friends down at Grambling State University—among them president Ralph Jones (second row, third from right) and coach Eddie Robinson (second row, right).

A slightly older version of me as a coach—feeling at home in the dugout during one of our games.

Being a scout means a lot of travel and a lot of note-taking, but it keeps me coming back to my favorite place—the ballpark.

Me with Toronto Blue Jays star Joe Carter, one of the many young players I've had the pleasure to scout and sign.

A young Bo Jackson (upper right) with a couple of old-timers from the Negro leagues—me, Monte Irvin (lower left), and Leon Day (lower right).

The Negro league reunion is always a good time. Here we are in 1980. Front row (from left to right): Gene Benson, Jimmy Crutchfield, Curt Thomas, Ray Dandridge, Effa Manley (owner of the Newark Eagles), Buck Leonard, Leon Day, Monte Irvin, Jake Stevenson, (and unidentified). Back row (from left to right): Quincy Trouppe, Bob Feller, me, Joe Black, "Old Soul" McDonald, Ted Paige, Judy Johnson, Chet Brewer, Chico Renfroe.

Me with Dewitt "Woody" Smallwood—a great man and a true friend. In addition to playing with Hank Aaron on the Indianapolis Clowns, Woody served as the first president of the Negro Leagues Baseball Museum. *(Credit: Phil Hardy)*

With Ken Burns, a good friend and the producer/director of the documentary *Baseball,* at the recently dedicated Buck O'Neil Baseball Complex in Sarasota, Florida.

Me and Ora, my beautiful wife of fifty years.

One of the proudest days of my life: In 1995, sixty-nine years after I cried in my mother's arms because I wasn't allowed to attend the all-white Sarasota High School, I finally received my diploma. And I know my Mama and Papa were there with me.

conducted himself with real class. One time in 1939, Clark Griffith called Josh and Buck into his office and told them he wanted them to be the first black players in the majors, but nothing ever came of it. When Buck was around forty, Bill Veeck offered to make him a St. Louis Brown, but to show you what kind of a guy Buck was, he declined because he knew the fans wouldn't be seeing the real Buck Leonard.

Buck is still with us, and he's our elder statesman, the greatest of us still alive. I remember him as a nice quiet man who would ride the bus or sit in the hotel lobby working crossword puzzles rather than going to the night spots. Buck Leonard was unique. He was probably the most studious man in the Negro leagues, and all the young ballplayers would come and talk with him.

Second Baseman: Newt Allen. Dick Seay, who played for the Newark Eagles, was a good hitter, but I'd pick Newt over him. Newt was stronger and had a better arm. Newt had a shortstop's arm. And quick, real quick he was.

Shortstop: People who remember Jackie Robinson as a second baseman might not be aware that Jackie was a shortstop in our league. Jesse Williams, who was our regular shortstop and a great one, willingly moved to second so that Jackie could play short for the Monarchs in 1945. Jesse was like that; he'd do anything that was asked of him. I'll have a lot more to say about Jackie in the next chapter. Strictly as a ballplayer, though, Jackie wasn't the best player in the Negro leagues when the Dodgers signed him, which isn't taking anything away from him, because with what he accomplished and what he went through, he proved he was the best man for the job. And he could play for me any time. *Any* time.

But I saw Honus Wagner play. I saw Pop Lloyd play. I love to watch Ozzie Smith play. Shortstop is the position the real students of the game like the best. And if I had to pick a shortstop for my team, it would be Willie Wells. Wee Willie was a lifetime .364 hitter with a .410 average against major league competition in barnstorming games. He could hit to all fields, hit with power, bunt, and stretch singles into doubles and doubles into triples. But it was his glove that truly dazzled. I told you about the play he made to rob me in the '42 East-West Game. Great as Ozzie Smith is, old-timers in St. Louis who saw Willie play for the St. Louis Stars still haven't seen his equal.

Willie, too, was one of the best baseball minds I ever knew. Like Buck Leonard, very, very intelligent. Even off the field, it just seemed like he was lost in thought. He was kind of a loner, not the type of guy who would be with the gang all the time. Willie, by the way, invented the batting helmet. When he was part of the Newark Eagles' "Million Dollar Infield," he got knocked unconscious by one of Bill Byrd's spitballs. Even though the doctor told him to sit out a few days, he came back the next day wearing a construction worker's helmet while he batted.

Third Baseman: Ray Dandridge. Now, here was a ballplayer's ballplayer. Ray would hang with the gang. He was going to be the last one to leave the clubhouse with the beer. On the field, they said a train would have a better chance of going through Ray's legs than a baseball, and I do believe they were right. I can still see him on those bowlegs of his—they called him Hooks—playing third in the '42 East-West Game. Monte Irvin says Brooks Robinson wasn't as good at third as Hooks was. With Willie Wells at short and Hooks at third, a grounder hit against the Eagles had no chance of surviving until the outfield. Ray could hit a little, too—line drives every which way.

Of all the guys who knocked on the door of the majors, Ray might have come the closest without actually getting in. The New York Giants signed him in 1949 when he was thirty-five—although Ray said he was twenty-nine—and in 1950 he hit .363 for the Minneapolis Millers and was named MVP. The fans up there loved him so much that they didn't want him to go to the majors. And the next year the Giants chose a young outfielder on the team over Ray, a guy who started his career with the Birmingham Black Barons. Guy by the name of Willie Mays.

Ray was very upset about that, but I look at it a little differently. Think about it: The Giants had Bobby Thomson to play third base. Although Ray could play, if you've got a guy twenty-seven years old you're not going to go out and get a guy who's thirty-five. And in those days, they would only have so many of us African-Americans on the team. I just wish Ray had been in another team's farm chain. You had to be in the right place at the right time when somebody needed you. Yeah, you had to be on time.

Leftfielder: You've heard me go on already about Turkey Stearnes, who talked to his bats. He could also make them sing. He had a .351 lifetime batting average to go along with his seven home run titles, and odd as he was, I would be more than happy to have both Turkey and his bat cases on my bus. The story goes that when Turkey was playing for the Los Angeles White Sox one winter, Bojangles Robinson came to the park and offered five dollars to any man who could hit a homer. Turkey hit four in one game, and Bojangles declared, "It's time for me to stop handing out money."

Centerfielder: He looked a little like Ruth, played a lot like Cobb, covered more ground than grass, and ran like the wind. If I had to name the best all-around player in the Negro leagues, I might just blurt out, "Oscar Charleston." He was everything. *Everything.* He was a charismatic figure, too, right from the day he joined his hometown Indianapolis ABCs in 1915 to 1954, the year he managed the Indianapolis Clowns to a championship—and died. He played on two of the best teams of all time, the 1931 Homestead Grays and the 1935 Pittsburgh Crawfords. Oscar McKinley Charleston wasn't afraid of a fight—he tangled with umpires, Ku Klux Klansmen, Cuban soldiers—but when it came to young players, he was a sweetheart, and we were always grateful for his counsel. This man not only encompassed the Negro leagues, this man *symbolized* the Negro leagues, with his heart and his spirit and his talent.

There's a *very* close second, though, and I can't get away from center field without mentioning Cool Papa Bell one more time. Now, you may have heard those incredible legends about Cool Papa, about how he was so fast he was once called out when his own batted ball hit him rounding first base, or about how he could hit the light switch and be in bed before the room went dark. People seem to think these are just the colorful folk tales of us old, jiving Negro-leaguers. But I'm here to tell you that one of those stories was true!

It happened when Cool Papa and Satchel were traveling with the Little Monarchs. They were staying in some hotel out West, and when Cool Papa checked into the room he noticed something funny: When he hit the off switch for the light, it took a few seconds before the light actually went out. Turn it on, and it went right on. But turn it off, and there was a delay. There must have been an electric short of some kind, and when Cool Papa discovered it, a light went on in his head.

That night he and Satchel got to talking as they headed up to the room. "Satchel," said Cool Papa, "am I still fast?" And Satchel said something like, "Cool Papa, you're fast, but you're close to forty and you're not as fast as you used to be." Cool Papa, of course, took great exception to Satchel's assessment, and after a little more arguing—they were in the room by then—he challenged Satchel to a bet. "I'll wager fifty I can turn the light switch off and get into bed before it goes dark."

Satchel should have known better, a sucker bet like that. But he said, "You're on."

It cost him fifty bucks to find out Cool Papa Bell was faster than the speed of light.

Rightfielder: You seldom see this name come up in all-time Negro league teams, maybe because he played a lot of first base, too. But every team needs a longball hitter, and my team would have Mule Suttles. When I say longball, I mean *long*ball. Mule was a coal miner from Alabama, and he swung a fifty-ounce bat. In Havana one time he hit a ball that was measured at six hundred feet, and they put a marker there to commemorate it. The biggest home run he ever hit—not the longest—was in the 1935 East-West Game, when he took Martin Dihigo deep with two outs and two on in the bottom of the eleventh. Whenever George—that was his given name—got to the plate, his teammates would yell, "Kick, Mule!" and kick it he did. Some say he hit sixty-nine homers in 1929. Babe Ruth holds the major league record with an .847 slugging percentage in 1920. Well, in 1926 for the St. Louis Stars, Mule had a slugging percentage of 1.000! He was part of that Newark infield with Wells and Dandridge for a while. A big jovial guy, he used to say, "Don't worry about the Mule going blind, just load the wagon and give me the lines." If you want to see what Mule looked like, go rent *I'm No Angel,* starring Mae West. Mule Suttles is in that.

Utility: He could've been considered for second base. He could've been considered for first base. He could've been one of the outfielders. He could even have walked in from the outfield to pitch a little relief, as he did so often. The most versatile player in the history of baseball was Martin Dihigo, *El Maestro.* After Johnny Mize played with him one year in the Dominican Republic, Mize said, "He was the only guy I ever saw who could play all nine positions, manage, run, and switch-hit. I thought I was having a pretty good year myself down there, and they were walking him to get to me." Handsome man, Dihigo was, tall, slender, good-looking. He's in the United States, Cuba, and Mexico Baseball Halls of Fame. Ended up working for Castro as the Minister of Sport. A very fine man, he was kind of quiet. You admired him because he wasn't a braggart, but you knew, and he knew, that he could do it all.

Pitchers: If I had one guy to start a game, it'd be—maybe you've heard of him—Satchel Paige. Give me a rotation, and I'd want Smokey Joe Williams; Slim Jones, who was a big tall left-hander for the Philadelphia Stars and the Lefty Grove of shadow ball; and my old roomie, Hilton Smith. I'd have to give Hilton plenty of work, though. Many's the time he'd come to the park and say, "Roomie, I feel good. I feel like I could throw the ball through the backstop," and sure enough, he'd get shelled. On the other hand, if he came to the park complaining about how tired his arm was, then I knew he was about to pitch a beauty.

Actually, of them all, Slim Jones may have turned out to be the best, but for a bad drinking habit that destroyed him. Slim, who looked a lot like Satchel and pitched like him, too, beat Satchel three times in 1936. But his drinking got so bad that, by 1938, he couldn't pitch anymore. They found him that winter frozen to death on a Philadelphia street, after he passed out from drinking. We had our tragic stories in the Negro leagues, that's for sure, and next to Josh's, Slim's was the saddest.

Now I'm going to give you a second team. My catcher—man, this is hard—would be Biz Mackey, the best pure defensive catcher we ever produced. I hate to leave out Louis Santop, who was also a great catcher, but Raleigh Mackey, who actually played on the same Hilldale team with Santop, was a wizard behind the plate.

First base is a difficult decision—no, I'm not going to pick Buck O'Neil; he'd be lucky to make the twelfth team. Luke Easter is my man. Luke played behind Buck Leonard with the Grays, then signed with the Cleveland Indians, for whom he hit .280 with twenty-eight homers in 1951. He might've been a big star if he hadn't broken his foot. He had real major-league power; we had some good hitters among the first basemen in our league, guys like Jim West and Showboat Thomas, but they couldn't hit the long ball like Luke. Luke was quite a guy, a big easygoing fellow. And actually, we wanted to get Luke away from the St. Louis Stars long before he went to the Grays, but he didn't want to leave home. He had a pretty good job there as a security guard. I know how Luke felt; I was hesitant myself to move away from my hometown. It wasn't until 1946 that I moved year-round to Kansas City, Missouri. Back home in Sarasota, I had a recreation hall for kids, and my dad and my brother ran it for me until I got home for the winter. But when I moved to Kansas City, I got a nice job at the post office. They told me, "Buck, whenever you want it, you got a job here." So I took it. And if it hadn't been for the scouting job I took with the Cubs and the same job I have now for the Royals, I'd probably have retired from the post office with a nice pension.

Anyway, getting back to my second team, at second base would be Dick Seay, as I mentioned. Shortstop would be Pop Lloyd, who was a little before my time—and that's saying something—but whom Connie Mack called the equal of Honus Wagner. Third base would be my old buddy Oliver Marcelle, who didn't need a nose to play great ball.

In the outfield, besides Cool Papa, we'd have Ted Strong and a marvelous hitter named Wild Bill Wright, who won our version of the Triple Crown in 1943, and when he retired he opened a restaurant in Mexico, where he also played for a time.

For pitchers, we could have Leon Day, Bullet Joe Rogan, Rube Foster's younger brother Willie, Ankleball Moss—I hated to hit against Ankleball, who died tragically in the middle of his career when he was shot by mistake during a dice game and a white doctor refused to treat him.

So many pitchers. So many players. So *many*. And here's the thing: If you took my second team, you just might beat my first team. And I could probably name a *third* team—Willard Brown, Judy Johnson, Roy Campanella, Larry Doby, Ernie Banks—that might be the best one of all.

Speaking of Roy Campanella, I strongly believe that, had Roy not become paralyzed in that awful car accident in '59, he would have been the first black manager in the majors. Roy had that squatty body, but that sucker was strong—and I think his personal strength helped him survive that accident. I wonder if many people know that, in a way, Campy *was* the first black manager in organized ball. When he was signed by the Dodgers in 1946 and was playing for their Nashua farm team in New Hampshire, Walt Alston was the manager. But one day Walt got thrown out of a game, and he handed the lineup card to Campy, which meant that, for just one day in 1946, white baseball had a black manager.

Yeah, we had some great players and some great characters. Oh, what a time it was. And I know that if you put any one of those teams on the field against an all-star team of major-leaguers from the same period, we'd more than likely win. It's just an estimate, and sometimes the competition wasn't so great, but in straight-up competition between major league and black ballclubs in the pre- and post-season, the black ballclubs won more than half the games. I've heard it said that we won because we had more to prove. That's true but it's also true that we didn't play as hard as we could for fear of inciting a riot. You're not going to cut or spike a major-leaguer, are you? No.

The Negro leagues wasn't all sportsmanship. We had some mean players. Sometimes you'd dress in the room next to the other team and hear them sharpening their spikes next door. "Hey, Buck," someone would shout through the wall. "Hear that? You tell your men to get out of the way." Alonzo Boone of the Cleveland Buckeyes, he would throw at you and it tickled him. He'd laugh at you, throw at you and laugh at you. His daddy was an umpire, too. I don't recollect a game in which he umpired while Alonzo pitched, but wouldn't that have been something?

Sugar Cornelius was mean. Plunk Drake was mean. Spoon Carter was mean. Me and Spoon roomed to-gether once on a barnstorming tour. The next year he was with Memphis, we were playing in Belleville, Illinois, and the first time up, I took him over the right field fence. The second time up, I took him over the left field fence. The next time up, I knew what was going to happen. I said, "Hold it, roomie. Hold it a minute while I get ready." Sure enough, he threw the ball right at my head, and I had to go down. "You trying to hit your old roomie?" I asked, and Spoon replied, "Buck, you hit me over the right field fence. You hit me over the left field fence. If I'm ever going to throw at you, wouldn't I throw at you now?" And I said, "I guess you're right."

We've gotten off the subject a little, the subject being major-leaguers versus Negro-leaguers. No, we never played as hard against them as we played against each other, and I suppose the same goes for them. To those who say the best players were in the majors, though, I say, "Bring 'em on."

Which reminds me of another Satchel story. At the end of the '46 season, I was with the Satchel Paige All-Stars on a tour against the Bob Feller All-Stars, and they ended up winning seven of the thirteen games. But Feller had players like Stan Musial, Ralph Kiner, Charlie Keller, Mickey Vernon, Phil Rizzuto, Johnny Sain, Bob Lemon—a regular all-star team. It was mostly Satchel and a bunch of us Monarchs; the big stars were either in winter ball or on a different barnstorming tour with Jackie Robinson.

We were in Los Angeles, and the stadium was packed. In the first inning, Rizzuto singled, Satchel struck out two guys with what he called his "thoughtful" stuff, and then up came Kiner, whom Satchel had never seen before—he played so much he didn't have time to keep up with what was going on in the rest of the baseball world. Well, Kiner blasted one of Satchel's fastballs over the fence for a two-run homer. "Who was that, Nancy?" Satchel asked me.

"That was Ralph Kiner," I said.

"Who's he?" said Satchel.

"Well, he led the National League in homers."

"Sure enough, Nancy. Just let me know when he comes up the next time."

When Kiner came up in the third inning, I yelled over to Satchel, "That's him!" And Satchel put him away with three quick pitches, strike one, strike two, strike three. As Kiner walked back to the dugout, Satchel smiled and said, "Nancy, I think we'd do real good if they let us play in them leagues."

Chapter 8

Now Hear This! Now Hear This!

In 1943 the Monarchs held spring training in Memphis. Our traveling secretary was Dizzy Dismukes, a wonderful pitcher in his day—I saw him pitch in Palm Beach long, long ago—and a college man who was an immense help to all the ballplayers in the club. Dizzy knocked on the door of my hotel room and invited me to come downstairs because there were some people he thought I should meet.

Well, the people were these three schoolteachers, all colleagues and friends of the wife of Bob Roberts, who owned the restaurant in the hotel. Now, people were always trying to set me up because, at thirty-one,

I really was pretty old to be a bachelor. Marriage wasn't something I ran away from, and I was plenty interested in the ladies; it's just that I wanted to see the world first before I settled down, and I hadn't found the woman I wanted to settle down with.

I found her that evening. As soon as I saw Ora Lee Owens, that was it! She was a pretty woman, but more than that, she was vibrant and open and smart. One of the ladies was leaving that night for Chicago, so after dinner we all went to the train station together to see her off, and then we went back to another of the girls' houses. We had a wonderful evening, and I began thinking that night that my bachelor days might be over.

I saw as much of Ora as I could that spring, and when I was named to the East-West Game, I invited her to Chicago to see me play. I didn't get any hits, but she got to see us win 2–1 behind the pitching of Satchel Paige, who, believe it or not, had a double in the game.

As luck would have it, the Monarchs played a number of games in Memphis that year, and I became acquainted with her folks. At first, they weren't too crazy about their daughter going out with a rootless and worldly ballplayer, the kind with a girlfriend in every city. Her father was a great, great man, a pure African who had been freed as a slave when he was twenty.

Without any education, he made a small fortune as a farmer, then lost it during the Depression. Still, he made sure that each of his four children was properly educated. Two of them became teachers and another became an assistant postmaster in Memphis. I guess I convinced them I was all right, because we got to be very close.

Don't forget, there was a war going on, and before too long, Willard Brown, Ted Strong, Connie Johnson, Joe Greene, and Ford Smith all went into the service. So the Monarchs fell on hard times, and with a few weeks to go in the season, my call came. I was drafted and assigned to the Navy Stevedore Battalion. Our job was to load and unload ships, first in the Mariana Islands and then at Subic Bay in the Philippines.

I'm not saying that prejudice was any worse in the Navy than it was in the outside world, but it seemed that way. In the Negro leagues, we could control our destiny; we knew which towns and hotels and restaurants would welcome us and which ones to avoid. But in the Navy, it was out of our hands. And what made it worse was that our own government, which was putting our lives on the line for freedom, was the one telling us to sit at the back of the bus. If I had captured a Japanese prisoner, I do believe the Navy would have treated him better than it did me.

A lot of the officers were whites from the South,

which didn't help race relations much. One of them
said to me, "It shouldn't bother you boys to say 'sir'
because you're accustomed to saying 'sir' to a white
man." He wasn't deliberately trying to insult me; he
was just calling it as he saw it.

Another time, we were taking some ammunition
out to a destroyer around five o'clock in the morning.
I was a bosun first class in charge of a crew of about a
dozen men, and up on the railing of the ship some
sailors were watching us. When reveille sounded, we
emerged from the hold and an officer leaned over the
railing and shouted, "Attention, niggers!" My men
froze when they heard this. We had all been called
nigger many times before, but this man was an officer
of the United States Navy, not some redneck in a
rusted-out pickup truck. I called up to him, "I believe
you could have addressed us a little better than that
. . . sir." And you know what he said? He said, "Oh,
I'm sorry." He *was* sorry, too. "Nigger" was such a
natural part of his vocabulary that it probably never
occurred to him that it was offensive. He was just
saying the sort of thing he had been saying all his life.

An ensign tried to pay me a compliment once. "I
like the way you handle your men, O'Neil," he said.
"If you were white, you'd be an officer by now." He
meant it as praise, but for me it was just a variation of
what so many players in the Negro leagues heard all

the time. "If only you were white . . ." Thank you very much, sir. That ensign could have made the injustice a little easier to swallow if he had said, "It's too bad the way things are, O'Neil, but one day the world is going to change." At least he would have given me a spoonful of hope.

Hope did come, in the person of a chaplain who passed through Subic Bay and told us about the work of the National Association for the Advancement of Colored People, about how they were slowly but surely bringing about changes in the Navy. Lord knew the Navy needed some changing! It would be another three or four years before President Truman integrated the Armed Forces. I knew a little about the NAACP, which was founded in 1910 when the Niagara Movement of W. E. B. DuBois was merged with white organizations concerned about racial injustice. But I never paid much attention to the NAACP until that chaplain told us about the changes they were fighting for and the successes they were having. I joined that day, and so did all the men in my group, and I've been active in the NAACP ever since. (In 1975 I was given a Life Membership, in 1988 I got a Heritage Membership, and today I serve on the board of the Kansas City chapter.)

One good thing about the Navy was that we were kept so busy and tired that we didn't have the time or the energy to feel homesick. Still, I did miss my family, and I especially ached for Ora, to whom I wrote every single day. After hundreds of letters, I finally got up the courage to ask her to marry me. It took a letter about two weeks to get to someone from Subic Bay and another two weeks for a reply, so for the next month, I was on pins and needles. Her first answer to my proposal was sweet, but basically she said that she would think about it. Well, at least she didn't say no. I don't know how much thinking she did, but it wasn't long before she wrote to say yes, she would marry me just as soon as I got out of the Navy. That really kept me going, because there were times when I thought World War II was never going to end.

I also got letters from my old friends back in Kansas City, Hilton and Wilkie and Tom Baird, who was a co-owner of the club. They kept me apprised of the fortunes—or rather misfortunes—of the Monarchs, who finished last in 1944 and had to rely on a lot of new players, and a lot of old ones, too. They also enclosed clippings from the black newspapers so I could keep up with the Negro leagues. (The Negro leagues didn't exist as far as *Stars and Stripes*, the service newspaper, was concerned.) Those letters were so sweet.

Hilton wrote to me about this one player he had recommended to the Monarchs, a football and track star at UCLA named Jack Roosevelt Robinson. The club actually did convince him to play shortstop for the 1945 season, and he did pretty good, batting .345, stealing a lot of bases and playing a decent shortstop. Jackie Robinson would electrify major league baseball in a few years, and he electrified the Monarchs in '45.

The electricity wasn't just on the field. He got them thinking in a different way. Growing up as he did in California, Jackie went to integrated schools and played on integrated teams. So when he got to the all-black Monarchs and saw the things they had to put up with—the Jim Crow laws, the separate drinking fountains and restrooms—he became furious. Othello "Chico" Renfroe, who played left field on that club, later told me that Jackie stormed out of so many places he left behind a fortune in change.

There was an incident in Muskogee, Oklahoma, that year that Hilton, who was Jackie's roommate, told me about. We had been buying gas for years at a service station there that had just one restroom—and we weren't allowed to use it. We thought nothing of it, and we gave the owner a lot of business anyway. Well, when the bus pulled into Muskogee and stopped at this station, Jackie got out and headed toward the restroom. The owner, who was filling the tank, called after him, "Hey boy! You know you can't go in there."

Jackie asked him why. "Because we don't allow no colored people in that restroom."

The guys knew about Jackie's hair-trigger temper, so they just stood around, wondering what he was going to do. Jackie turned to the man very calmly and said, "Take the hose out of the tank." The owner stopped the pump and looked at him. "Take the hose out of the tank," Jackie repeated. Then he turned to his teammates and said, "Let's go. We don't want his gas."

Well, the Monarchs had two fifty-gallon tanks on the bus. That gas station wasn't going to sell a hundred gallons of gas to one customer until the bus came back through a few weeks later. He shoved the hose back into the tank and said, "All right, you boys can use the restroom. But don't stay long."

From then on, the Monarchs could use the restroom whenever they passed through. But more importantly, they decided never to patronize any gas station or restaurant where they couldn't use the facilities.

But I missed all of that, because me and my men were loading and unloading—tote that barge, lift that bale—in Subic Bay. In late October of 1945, at around eleven o'clock at night, I heard this summons from the commanding officer over the loudspeaker: "John O'Neil, please report to my office immediately."

I didn't know what he could want. But when I got to

his office, this white man looked me in the eye and told me, "I just thought you should know that the Brooklyn Dodgers have just signed Jackie Robinson. He's going to play for their minor league team in Montreal next year." Well, I thanked the officer for this information, then got on the horn myself:

"Now hear this! Now hear this! The Dodgers just signed Jackie Robinson!"

You should have heard the celebration. Halfway around the world from Brooklyn, we started hollering and shouting and firing our guns into the air. I don't know that we made that much noise on VJ Day.

This was progress. The Dodgers signing Jackie wasn't just about baseball or about opportunities for the Negro-leaguers. This was progress for the whole country. It didn't matter who was the first or which team had the courage; this was the first real step toward integration, toward equality, since maybe Reconstruction. Jackie hadn't played an inning yet in what they called organized baseball—a team I disliked because it implied the Negro leagues were *dis*organized—but we knew when we heard the news of his signing that night in the Philippines that this was the dawning of a new era. No more shadow ball. No more shadow America.

Writers like Sam Lacy of the *Baltimore Afro-American* and Wendell Smith of the *Pittsburgh Cou-*

BUCK O'NEIL

rier had been crusading against the color barrier for
years. Their biggest obstacle was the commissioner of
baseball himself, Kenesaw Mountain Landis, a judge
who publicly maintained there was no discrimination
in baseball and privately worked against any effort to
end discrimination. When Bill Veeck tried to buy the
Philadelphia Phillies in 1943, Landis awarded the
franchise to a gambler, knowing that Veeck planned to
field a team of Negro-leaguers. Landis might have been
a great man in some regards, but he did all of us a
favor when he died in 1944. When Ric Roberts of the
Pittsburgh Courier asked the newly named commissioner, Happy Chandler, "What about black boys?"
Chandler answered, "If they can fight and die in Oki-
nawa, Guadalcanal, in the South Pacific, they can play
baseball in America." But those were just words until
Branch Rickey found Jackie Robinson.

I knew that, unlike many other people in the majors, Rickey was serious about integration, that it
wasn't just hot air. See, before that, there'd be rumors
about tryouts for our boys. Josh and Buck Leonard and
Chico Renfroe and even Jackie Robinson, they'd all
been given tryouts, but it was just a show. The only
reason the owners bothered was that sportswriters like
Smith and Lacy and even some white writers like
Jimmy Powers and Shirley Povich were pressuring
them to do it. So they said, well, here's what we'll do:

To quiet that talk down, we'll bring in some guys and put them through this charade, and then say these guys weren't good enough. And the white public wanted to believe that anyway.

Rickey was different. He stuck his neck out on the line, because a lot of people wanted him to fail. There were a couple of white owners who were making a lot of money off of black baseball. The Washington Senators' Clark Griffith was making a killing, because the Homestead Grays played in Griffith Stadium when the Senators were out of town. We would go in there and play the Grays and fill up the place; the Senators would come home and play any club other than the Yankees and they'd have twelve thousand people in there. We had 'em hanging from the rafters. So he was probably making $100,000 off the rent and the concessions with the Grays.

Same with the Yankees; we played those great four-team doubleheaders in Yankee Stadium, and when we filled the ballpark up, the Yankees got a percentage of the gate, all the concessions, and all the parking. We also played in the Yankees' minor league ballparks in Newark and Kansas City; they were getting the concessions in all of them, and this was a strong incentive not to integrate. In fact, because Judge Landis was such an imposing force against it, I believe that if Landis had still been alive in 1945, Rickey wouldn't have signed Jackie. It just would've been too difficult to get it through. Rickey was ready to do it before then, but Landis was in the way.

Some people argued that the pace of integration was too fast. Let me tell you something: Integration would have been too damn slow in arriving even if it had happened right after the Civil War. That's how we all felt. Maybe that's why, when it did happen, a hundred years too late, there were some nitpickers among us who thought players other than Jackie should have been the first. And I'm not even talking about Satchel or Josh or Buck Leonard. Many of the Monarchs felt our young pitcher Connie Johnson should have been first. Ted Strong, Willard Brown, Bonnie Serrell—all of these guys were deserving. Back East, they might've been surprised it wasn't Monte Irvin or Roy Campanella. Bonnie, whom Hilton Smith thought was a better player than Jackie, was so disappointed that he went to Mexico to play and never came back.

As for Satchel, who for many whites was the only black ballplayer they knew of, I know he was kind of upset that he wasn't the one, and that opens up an interesting subject. I told you before about how torn Satchel was, but even with the reservations he had, when the time came he felt insulted. What he was saying was, I don't know why in the hell you could take that guy before you take me. I'm Satchel Paige. It was his pride that hurt.

Now, maybe that was unreasonable because of Satchel's age and all, but I will say this: If it had been ten years earlier, he *would* have been the first.

There are people who think Satchel was too outspoken to have handled the job like Jackie did. I have a different opinion. I don't think he would have had as tough a time as Jackie did! Satchel was a superstar, and the whole country knew about him, even people who hadn't ever seen him pitch. If Satchel had been the first, people would have seen him as an individual, an established star; people saw Jackie as a symbol, as a black man. Satchel was just Satchel, and he'd have had an easier time of it. If he would have said something outspoken, people wouldn't have resented it as much as if Jackie said it. They would have said, well, that's Satchel Paige. But with Jackie, they would have said, he wants to be a smartass nigger.

See, Jackie was under pressure every minute. That's why Branch Rickey picked him, because Jackie had been under pressure all his life, and the amazing thing was that, knowing Jackie's disposition, he did take the things he took. Because Jackie was fiery. But take it he did—and I firmly believe that was what killed him at such an early age. Jackie aged faster than any man I've ever seen. He died a young man, only fifty-two.

Satchel, on the other hand, was never under any pressure. Satchel didn't know the meaning of the word pressure.

I'll tell you another guy who was hurt that he didn't get the call: Josh Gibson. By the time Jackie was signed, it was too late for Josh, and he never got over the fact that he didn't get the chance ten years earlier, when he was the best hitter in the game. People say that killed him, broke his heart, but I won't go that far because there was much more to it; Josh seemed destined to live in pain and disappointment. His wife had died giving birth to twins early in his career—his son, Josh, Jr., played for the Homestead Grays for a year in the fifties—and people say he never got over that.

But as long as he could play, Josh could get over anything, at least while he was on the field. He even lived with a brain tumor. Josh played for years with a tumor in his head that caused him terrible headaches and mental breakdowns. Actually, I don't even think Josh knew he was so sick. He knew something was wrong with him, but we didn't have team doctors back then. If Josh had been playing in the majors, they'd have had a doctor examine him, find out what was wrong, but he didn't know he had a brain tumor until he was damn near dead.

By then, around '46, we could see the change in him. He had gained quite a bit of weight. In spite of his troubles, Josh had always been a very jovial guy, but toward the end he was kind of mean at times. And I guess he was doped up, because one time he started talking to me about our old days on the Grays, and I realized he thought I was Buck Leonard. It was just a heartbreaking thing to see.

People have said all kinds of things about what happened to Josh, that he was a heavy drinker and a drug user. But I believe the drugs involved were more or less painkillers. And I don't believe he started drinking all that much, because Josh wasn't that big of a drinker. He was a social drinker like the rest of us, but he was no drunk.

Anyway, whatever happened, Josh died of a stroke on January 20, 1947, only three months before Jackie Robinson came to Brooklyn and changed the world. Josh might not have been the first black big-leaguer, but there was no greater catcher in the Negro leagues, or the major leagues for that matter. Of all the sad stories of the Negro leagues, Josh's was the saddest of all.

In the end, everybody realized that Branch Rickey took the right man in Jackie. Rickey might have chosen an easygoing player with talent equal to Jackie's, an unflappable sort of guy who didn't let things get under his skin, but believe me, easygoing wouldn't have done it. I was easygoing and I couldn't have done it. Jackie was chosen precisely because he was fiery and, above all, intelligent enough to know he couldn't lose his temper.

In their first meeting, when Rickey told Jackie he would have to turn the other cheek, Jackie asked him, "Are you looking for someone who would not have the courage to fight back?" And Rickey answered him, "I am looking for someone with the courage *not* to fight back!" And Jackie was that someone.

I can honestly say I felt no envy toward Jackie. I had no illusions—I was thirty-four and rounding third. Even in my prime, I might not have made it in an era of big, power-hitting first basemen like Jimmie Foxx, Hank Greenberg, Johnny Mize. Like I always say, shed no tears for me.

The war might have been over, but our work in the Stevedore Battalion wasn't. If anything, me and my men worked harder after the Japanese surrendered than we did before, loading all the ships for their return home. I was dead tired when I finally mustered out of the Navy in St. Louis in 1946.

I wasn't too tired, though, to go to Memphis, where Ora and I were married. We spent the winter with my family in Sarasota, and after spring training, we moved to Kansas City. I knew I was married because for the first time in my career with the Monarchs, I didn't check into the Streets Hotel. Frank Duncan had some little kitchenette apartments over on Prospect Avenue, and that's where we lived our first year of marriage. (Later on, we moved into the duplex apartment on 11th Street where Dizzy Dismukes lived.) Ora already had a bachelor's degree in education from LeMoyne College in Tennessee, and thanks to Tom Baird, she was able to get a teaching position over in Kansas City, Kansas.

The world was a different, better place after the war, and my life was a different, better life. It means so much to go through life with a partner, someone with whom you can share your triumphs and disappointments.

As it turned out, marriage did a world of good for my batting average as well as my soul. In 1946 I led the American League in hitting with a .350 average, just two points above Willard Brown. The reassembled Monarchs were intent on reclaiming the championship of black baseball that season. We were also energized by all the people who came out to see the team Jackie Robinson had played on the year before. Jackie, you see, was the big news of '46, and the pages of the black newspapers—the front pages—were filled with accounts of his exploits with the Montreal Royals. The scouts were there, too, looking for the next Jackie Robinson, and that inspired us. And so now we were being discovered yet again, as the team Jackie

Robinson came from. Funny thing was, no one realized that this was the beginning of the end for the Negro leagues, because 1946 was the Negro leagues' best season financially. We were really packing them in and everybody was making money.

Certainly we didn't realize it, because we walked away with the pennant in '46 and we felt pretty good about things. We were back in the Negro World Series, against the Newark Eagles, who had an easy time of it over in the Negro National League. Biz Mackey had an outstanding club, with Larry Doby, Monte Irvin, Ray Dandridge, Leon Day, and another great pitcher named Max Manning, who went undefeated in league games that year.

But we still had a great club, and we still had Satchel—or at least we thought we did.

Satchel was still with the Monarchs, but he was with us less and less, because Wilkie would send him to so many different places, lending him out for a cut of the gate. J.L. even had a private plane just for Satchel, a DC-10, and Wilkie's son Dick was the pilot. But the fact is that even Satchel Paige wasn't bigger than the Negro leagues by 1946. I think Satchel learned that back in '44, at the East-West Game, when Satchel wanted to stick up the promoters for more money and they said no. What the owners knew, what they finally found out, was that no one ballplayer was bringing people to the game—it was the game itself. So Satchel walked out on the East-West Game and never came back, and it didn't matter. Nobody stayed away from Comiskey Park because Satchel wouldn't be there.

But we needed Satchel to be there against Newark, and he was. Fact is, Satchel even went nine innings to clinch the pennant for us against the Clowns. Satchel always wanted to dominate the big games. Unfortunately, this time it didn't go as he had planned it.

The Series started at the Polo Grounds, and Hilton Smith went out there in the first game and led 1–0 going to the sixth. Then Satchel came in—and gave up the tying run on a hit by Johnny Davis. Satchel was so mad he went up and got a base hit the next inning and came home on an error and a hit. That held up and we won 2–1, beating Leon Day, who also pitched great.

That got us off on the right foot, but then came the second game, in Newark's Ruppert Stadium. Joe Louis was there and threw out the first ball, and then the Eagles threw us for a loop when they roughed up Satchel and won 7–4.

So it was all even now, and it stayed that way after two games in Kansas City. We won 15–5 behind big Hank Thompson's four hits, but then we lost 8–1, with Satchel giving up a three-run home run to Monte Irvin. Seeing how Satchel had been victimized in three games, I figured he'd be raring to get revenge. I had no idea that would be the last I'd see of Satchel that season.

We went to Chicago for the fifth game, and Hilton was magnificent, handing Manning his first defeat of the season as we won 5–1 to go up three games to two.

Now we needed only one win, but we had to go back to Newark for the sixth and seventh games. And as much as we looked for Satchel, we couldn't find him. When I hit a homer and then Willard Brown hit one in game six, we were hoping maybe we wouldn't need him, but Monte beat us both by hitting two out of the park, and we lost, 9–7.

Before the seventh and deciding game, we were changing in the visitors' clubhouse when Frank Duncan came in and asked, "Anybody seen Willard and Ted?" Satchel was still AWOL, but now Willard Brown and Ted Strong were missing, too. The story we got was that they had gone into New York that morning to sign winter ball contracts with the Puerto Rican League and they hadn't gotten back. Then Dunc asked, "And where's Satchel? Doesn't he know he's supposed to be starting this game?" Satchel was probably messing around in New York, figuring the game wouldn't start without him.

Willard and Ted didn't show up until the game was

almost over, saying they'd gotten caught in traffic. Satchel? He didn't show up at all.

I know this sounds crazy—I warned you that it would—but to Willard and Ted, negotiating a winter contract was more important than the ballgame, game seven or not, because they were trying to make a living, and now they knew they were going to work all winter. And Satchel . . . well, you know, Satchel was used to showing up late. Remember the last game of the '42 Negro World Series, when he was paying off a speeding ticket in a barbershop? Listen, I can talk about Satchel all day and all night and never be able to explain him. But, of course, we were all very disappointed in him.

So, because of all this craziness, we had to go with Ford Smith on the mound, which actually didn't upset us at all because Ford was a good pitcher and Satchel hadn't exactly been overpowering against the Eagles. We also had to go with Hilton and Joe Greene, usually our catcher, in the outfield instead of Willard and Ted. All great players, but there we were, trying to play the seventh game of the World Series without Satchel Paige and two other guys I think belong in the Hall of Fame. And things looked pretty bad for us—mainly thanks to me. We were ahead 2–1 late in the game when I muffed an easy grounder. It hit a pebble but I still should have caught it, only it went right through my legs. That would have been the third out of the inning, but then Larry Doby walked, Monte Irvin walked, and Johnny Davis doubled them both in to put Newark up 3–2.

Actually, we were doing well to be down only 3–2 to Max Manning in the top of the ninth. One of our runs had come on my second homer of the series, which matched my home run total for the entire season. Like I've said, I was not the most prodigious hitter in baseball. So when I came up with two on and two out, I was wondering, am I on a tear? Or have I shot my wad?

I got a pitch from Manning I liked and I heard the sound of the ball hitting the sweet spot of my bat. As I raced down the first base line, I could hear the Monarchs shouting for joy. The ball was heading for the deepest part of the ballpark in center field, and as I rounded first, I began thinking I might have an inside-the-park homer, or at least a triple.

Leon Day, however, was on his horse. As good a pitcher as Leon was, he might have been a better centerfielder. I don't know how he did it, but he ran that ball down and made an amazing catch, better even than the one Willie Mays made on Vic Wertz in the 1954 World Series. Everyone on our bench just stood there, their mouths hanging open. Leon Day had saved the day for Newark.

Thinking back on that ball I hit, I see it as sort of a symbol for my career. Like that ball, I went a long way, and like that ball, I came close to making it over the wall. Alas, I didn't make it, not as a player anyway. But you know what? I felt good because I had given it my best shot.

Actually, you could also say there was something symbolic about those three guys missing the game. At that point, even though the Negro leagues had had their best season—clearing two million dollars in profit for the first time that year—it was true that most guys had their sights set on other things than black baseball. Jackie Robinson had played well in the minors, and while everyone was thrilled that Jackie would be coming to the majors soon, this meant the Negro leagues weren't going to be as important as they had been.

I was looking ahead myself during the Series, to the biggest barnstorming tour ever, when Satchel Paige and Bob Feller were going to square off against each other with their own all-star teams in games all across the country. I was excited to be chosen for the Satchel Paige All-Stars, along with guys like Hilton Smith, Gene Benson, and Quincy Trouppe, because I knew I'd be making more money in one month than I had made in the last six. And I was excited to be able to play against guys like Mickey Vernon, Phil Rizzuto, Johnny Sain, and Stan Musial, who came in when we were in Los Angeles right after the big-league World Series.

But I may have been most excited about taking my first plane ride, since both teams traveled in DC-10s, just like Satchel had been doing for some time. That's when we found out how the other half lived.

I also felt that, even though it was black against white, this tour was an event that could have a real effect on big-league integration, because it took place after Jackie had proven himself, and if a lot of us weren't that lucky, we could at least prove ourselves against big-leaguers in these games. Even though the white owners didn't like these games, some of the biggest major-leaguers wanted to play us, were all for us. Heck, Bob Feller found out that he couldn't do what Satchel, at age forty, was doing. Satchel could still pitch the first three innings of every game, day after day; when Feller tried to do that, he almost hurt his arm. Satchel made his case for being a big-leaguer right there. So did Hank Thompson, who was our big gun on the tour.

For the rest of us who didn't quite get that chance, though, the Negro leagues were our salvation. For me, it gave me almost ten more years of pride.

Chapter 9

Long Live the Monarchs

Ever since I saw Rube Foster use smoke signals to control a game, I had been fascinated by the job of the baseball manager, and in 1948 I got my chance to be one.

Actually, I had a chance the year before, but the timing and the circumstances weren't right. Dick Wilkinson, Wilkie's son, was upset when we lost a game late in the season to the Clowns in Indianapolis, and he wanted to fire Frank Duncan right there on the spot. He took the keys for the bus from Frank and tried to hand them to me. "Heck, no," I said. "I don't want those keys."

"Are you going to manage this ballclub?" Dick asked.

"No, I'm not going to manage this ballclub. You want to get rid of Frank, that's your business. But you're going to have to wait until you get back to Kansas City and your daddy and Frank can talk. This is Frank Duncan's job. I don't want it."

When Dick asked Hilton Smith to take over, Hilton turned him down, too, so Frank kept his job until the season was completed. You couldn't really blame Dick. The Monarchs weren't a particularly strong team in '47, and he might have been a little frantic because he—and his father and a lot of other people—knew they were seeing the beginning of the end of the Negro leagues. We lost Willard Brown and Hank Thompson to the St. Louis Browns that year. Worse, when the Brooklyn Dodgers and Jackie Robinson traveled to St. Louis to play the Cardinals in '47, half our fans went with them.

The eastern Negro National League teams were hurt even worse. Attendance for the Newark Eagles went from 120,000 to 57,000, and when Effa Manley, the Eagles' owner, complained, she was reprimanded by the *Kansas City Call*, which wrote, "The day of loyalty to Jim Crow anything is fast passing away. Sister, haven't you heard the news? Democracy is a-coming, fast." The *Call* was half right, half wrong: The death

of the Negro leagues might have been a necessary sacrifice as a tradeoff for integration, but democracy,
though it was a-coming, didn't move very fast.

For Willard Brown, it didn't move at all. Willard
could play rings around most of the guys who were on
that Browns team, but he didn't do much in St. Louis,
because they didn't give him a chance to play. They
were so screwed up on that ballclub. Willard told me
about the time he hit a home run—and, like I told you,
he hit the first homer by a black player in the American League. Willard had borrowed another guy's bat
before he hit. So then Willard came back to the dugout, and when he got back, he saw the guy he borrowed the bat from break the bat! He didn't want it
back after a black guy had used it. Those were the
kind of guys they had on that team.

The whole attitude in St. Louis was different than it
was in Brooklyn with Rickey and the Dodgers. The
Browns were only interested in boosting the gate by
bringing in Willard and Hank, and they didn't have a
good enough team to compete with the Cardinals for
the fans in St. Louis. The Browns were on the bottom
of the totem pole. Another real problem was that the
Browns were going to have to pay the Monarchs some
more money if those two guys lasted out the season,
so they just released them before the season ended.

Willard was bitter, you can believe that. He knew

that at twenty-eight he'd never get another crack at the big leagues. He later went to the Texas League, and he was always welcome to play for me in Kansas City, but he never got another shot at the majors. At least Hank Thompson, who hit .256 in St. Louis, was given another chance, and Hank played for five years or so with the New York Giants and helped them win a pennant in 1951 with eight homers down the stretch. Somebody was smart enough not to leave Hank out in the cold.

Black baseball wasn't yet dead in '48, although Wilkie did sell his share of the club to Tom Baird. It was Baird who asked me to become a player-manager. I could still get the wood on the ball, but I didn't flatter myself; I was thirty-six, and I knew I was at the end of my playing career. Besides, most Negro league teams had player-managers as a sort of cost-saving thing—for one salary, you could get a man to play two roles.

The key was in keeping the two roles separate. That lesson was imparted to me right away by Dizzy Dismukes, our traveling secretary. It's funny how some people weave themselves throughout your life. When I was a kid, I had seen a great submarine pitcher for the Indianapolis ABCs named Dizzy Dismukes, and when I became a Monarch for the first time, that same man showed me the ropes. Dizzy was anything but dizzy. Once his playing days were over, he became a manager, a sportswriter, the secretary of the Negro National League, and after the Negro leagues died, a scout.

Anyway, when Dizzy and I were drawing up the rooming assignments that first year, he told me, "Buck, you can't stay with Hilton anymore."

When I asked him why, he said, "I know you and Hilton are friends, but now you are the manager. If you're staying with Hilton and doing a lot of things with him, it's going to look like you're showing him a preference. You can't have anybody, even the least important guy on the team, think that you're showing a preference for another ballplayer. You stay by yourself."

"It's going to be mighty lonely," I said. "I'm used to having a roommate."

"You'll get used to it. Besides, now that you're the manager, you're gonna be spending all your free time with me. Your job doesn't end at the ninth inning anymore."

Indeed it didn't. When the game was over, I had to think about expenses, schedules, travel arrangements, personnel decisions. One night when I suggested to Diz that we go over some things at one of our favorite night spots, he said, "You can't go there, Buck. The players go there, and you don't want to cramp their style. Besides, you might see something you don't want to see." The most important thing that Dizzy taught me, though, was that while you have to think of all players as equals, you can't treat every player the same way. Some guys need pats on the back, some guys need kicks in the butt, and some guys just plain need to be left alone. And some guys need all three.

I always considered myself a manager's player, so naturally I became something of a player's manager. A sportswriter once referred to my approach as a "soft-hand policy." But I was tough when I had to be, and aggressive and enthusiastic once the game started. The one and only time I ever got thrown out of a game was when an umpire forgot, or hadn't learned, a certain rule. It happened in a game against the Clowns, and with runners on first and second, their batter bunted the ball into the air. I let the ball drop and then threw to second to start a double play, but the umpire imposed the infield fly rule. Now, I knew that you couldn't have the infield fly rule on an attempted bunt, but he didn't, and when I got a little hot about his ignorance, he tossed me out of the game. For the most part, though, I had the utmost respect for umpires, who were only doing their job on a part-time basis. Many of the Negro league umps had been fine players—Bullet Joe Rogan, Hurley McNair, Frank Duncan—fine men like that.

I do believe it was easier to be a manager back in those days than it is today. The modern ballplayer has more of a life outside the ballpark. Baseball was *all* we had. We ate, drank, breathed, and slept baseball. If we had an all-night bus ride, we stayed up and talked about the game we had just played, the mistakes we made, the pitches they hit, the pitches we missed. I generally assigned roommates by position, catcher with catcher, pitcher with pitcher, shortstop with second baseman. I once came into the room of Bonnie Serrell and Jesse Williams and saw them passing the baseball off to one another.

How, you might want to ask, did I manage my good friend, Satchel Paige? Actually, he was snatched away from the Monarchs in midseason my first year, having signed with Bill Veeck's Cleveland Indians. He came back in 1950, then went off to the St. Louis Browns for three seasons, only to return in '55. So he never really tried my patience to the extent he had tried other managers'. Besides, he knew me and I knew him. The key was to get him to the ballpark on time. Satchel always drove his own car, and his sense of direction was terrible, so I had one of the younger players—the older ones were too smart or too scared to drive with Satch—keep him company, watch the clock and navigate. Without someone to read a map and look for signs, Satchel was liable to wind up anywhere.

I never ordered Satchel to do anything or threatened him if he didn't, because demands rolled off him like water off a duck's back. I did, however, occasionally con him. One time we were traveling to Kankakee, Illinois, and Satchel was scheduled to start the game. Fortunately, there was a lake in Kankakee, so I said, "Satch, I'll tell you what. There's some good fishing in Kankakee. You get there early enough, and we can drop that hook."

"Hey, Nancy," he said. "I like that! What time are you guys leaving?"

"Eight o'clock sharp."

"Great! Be sure to get me up."

And he was up with everyone else, rarin' to go.

I wanted to win as much as anyone—we did finish first in '50, '51, and '53—but it soon became apparent that our survival didn't depend on victories. Rather, it depended on producing ballplayers for the major leagues. The ballclub would get a bonus, maybe five thousand dollars, if we found a player that a major league team thought was worth signing, and by and large they were looking for young players they could develop in their farm systems. So we had to let some good players go, very good players, because they were thirty and over, while we kept some unproven, unfinished kids.

A case in point was this young catcher from St.

Louis, fresh out of high school. Dizzy had heard about him, scouted him, and signed him for us. He was big and strong, and he was a nice kid from a good family. In 1938 he might not have made the Monarchs as a catcher (he wasn't as good as Joe Greene) or as an outfielder (he couldn't have beaten out Willard Brown or Ted Strong), but in 1948 he was just the kind of player we were looking for. His name was Elston Howard.

We had Earl Taborn as our catcher at the time, but when I saw Elston hit one over the scoreboard at Municipal Stadium in his first game, I found a place for him in the outfield. Later, when Taborn left to try out for the majors, I put Elston behind the plate. When Tom Greenwade, the scout for the Yankees who signed Mickey Mantle, came through in 1950 to check out Willard Brown, I told him, "Willard can play for your club, but the player you should be looking at is our young catcher. He can play the outfield, too, and besides, he's a fine person." So that's how Elston became the first African-American to play for the Yankees.

We came upon our biggest find in 1949. Cool Papa Bell was managing the Little Monarchs, the B team that had been formed for Satchel, and when he came back from a trip, he started raving about this seventeen-year-old shortstop he had seen playing for the Black Sheepherders out of San Antonio. Cool had seen him play in several games and loved his power and potential, so that winter I drove to Dallas and signed him up, even though I had never seen him swing a bat. Cool's word was good enough for me. Turns out it was good enough for the Hall of Fame. The young man was Ernie Banks.

Ernie has been kind enough over the years to credit me with his positive outlook on life, but I have to say he was a delight right from the start, on the field and off. He didn't demonstrate his tremendous power in 1950, his first season with us, but after a two-year stint in the Army he came back and drove in forty-seven runs in just forty-six games. He was hardly a secret anymore. John Donaldson tried to get the White Sox to sign him, but when a white scout overruled him, John told them to take the job and shove it.

Ernie and I both went to Chicago for the 1953 East-West Game at Comiskey Park, where he was the shortstop for the West and I was the manager. Late in the game, when the score was tied, Dr. J. B. Martin, the owner of the Memphis Red Sox, who was sitting in the box next to the dugout, leaned over and said to me, "Buck, I think we might need another dozen balls." The East squad was supposed to furnish the balls that year, but it was running low, and Doc knew I always carried a dozen or two extra balls on our bus.

But Ernie was coming to bat, so I said, "No, Doc. I don't think we're going to need any more because this kid is going to hit the ball out of the ballpark." And sure enough, he did. Doc Martin thought I was a swami. What I knew was that Ernie Banks was destined for greatness.

After the game, Tom Baird called me and told me to bring Ernie to Wrigley Field the next morning. When we got there, Wid Matthews, the Cubs' general manager, said, "Buck, I'll tell you what. Tom is going to sell his ballclub pretty soon because that baseball of yours is just about over. When he does, we want you to come to work for us." I thanked him, and then he said, "You signed Ernie to a contract with the Kansas City Monarchs. Your first assignment as a scout with us will be to sign him to a contract with the Chicago Cubs." So I got to sign Ernie twice.

All in all, the Monarchs sent seventeen players to the majors. None were as good as Banks, but how's this for an all-star team of the players I wrote down on my lineup card: Elston Howard, catcher; Pancho Herrera, first base; Gene Baker, second base; Ernie Banks, shortstop; Hank Thompson, third base; George Altman, Lou Johnson, and Bob Thurman, outfield; Satchel Paige, Connie Johnson, and Hank Mason, pitchers. Wid Matthews later showed me a letter he got from a fan, complaining about the Cubs signing

Baker, Banks, Altman, Johnson, pitcher Bill Dickey, etc. "What are you trying to do?" read the letter. "Make the Cubs look like the Kansas City Monarchs?"

Even though attendance was dwindling and teams were disappearing, some great talent passed through the Negro leagues in the early fifties. You just had to look fast or you might miss them. The Birmingham Black Barons had this seventeen-year-old outfielder with the most spectacular arm I had ever seen. Joe Greene was tagged up at third ready to score on a routine sacrifice fly ball, but when he got to the plate, Pepper Bassett, their catcher, already had the ball in his hand, freshly thrown in from center by Willie Mays. (The Red Sox, who owned the stadium the Barons played in, had the inside track on Mays, and they sent one of their scouts to see him, but the game was rained out, so the scout went home rather than wait around another day and be inconvenienced by a Negro. The Giants signed him instead.)

In the spring of '52, the Monarchs and the Clowns played a few preseason games together, and one day Buster Haywood, the Indianapolis manager, inserted a shortstop I had never heard of in the fourth spot in the order, where catcher Piggy Sands usually hit. "Who's this kid?" I asked Buster.

"You'll see," he said.

Intrigued, I instructed our starting pitcher, Ford

Smith, to give the cleanup hitter his best fastball. Well, this 160-pound kid hit the ball up against the right field fence. I saw Buster over in the Clowns' dugout, looking over at me with an enormous grin on his face. I told my next pitcher, a hard-throwing righthander named Booker McDaniels, to give the kid a *good* fastball. Sure enough, the shortstop lined the ball over the centerfielder's head so that it, too, hit the wall. Now Buster's grin grew even larger.

My third and last pitcher was Gene Collins, a southpaw with outstanding stuff. I wanted to see what the kid would do against a left-hander's curveballs, so I instructed Gene to throw him some breaking balls. His third pitch wound up over the left field fence, and Buster's face could hardly contain his smile. Henry Aaron could hit, all right.

Buster and I were eating supper that night, and he was just as proud as a peacock over his new shortstop. He was going on and on about what this Aaron kid was going to do to the Monarch pitching staff during the season. I just sat there listening, smiling and listening, listening and smiling, until my grin got as big as Buster's did after Aaron's homer. "Buck," he said, "what have you got to smile about, after what the kid did to you today?"

"Buster," I said, "when you come to Kansas City to play us again, Henry Aaron won't be on your ballclub." Sure enough, when the Clowns came to Kansas City a few weeks later, Aaron was the property of the Boston Braves.

I had the pleasure of signing Ernie Banks and Lou Brock, two Hall-of-Famers, and Lee Smith and Joe Carter, two future Hall-of-Famers. But I had another one slip through my fingers. In the early fifties, the Monarchs played a game in Omaha, and the head of the YMCA there brought around a young man, a baseball and basketball player from Creighton University. I talked to him in our dugout for a while, and finally I asked him if he would like to play for the Monarchs. "Thanks for the offer, Mr. O'Neil," said Bob Gibson, "but I'm hoping to play ball for the St. Louis Cardinals."

That told me something. A few years before, Bob Gibson might have jumped at the chance to play for the Kansas City Monarchs. But Negro baseball was no longer the glorious enterprise it had once been. In 1954 our highest-paid player was actually a woman. Forgive me, Ora, I don't intend to demean women, but we had signed Toni Stone away from the Indianapolis Clowns not because she was the best second baseman around but because she could give us a boost at the gate.

Toni was a pretty fair player, having played on her

high school baseball team in Minnesota. She ran well, and she knew what she was doing around the bag. But she wasn't of the same caliber as our other players, and the pitchers did take it easy on her when the game wasn't on the line. There wasn't much resentment that I can recall; I think teammates and opponents knew the league was fighting for survival. The Monarchs certainly had no problem with Toni. They respected her, and she usually dressed in my office while I dressed in the regular clubhouse. She later married an attorney and moved to San Francisco. At least I can claim the distinction of having managed a coed baseball team.

Toward the end, the league got so raggedy that I used myself as a pitcher. In '53 we were in a pennant race, and we had a big series coming up in Memphis. But first we had to play two games against a semipro team in Wichita. I wanted to save my pitchers, so I came in to relieve in the eighth inning of the first game, and lo and behold, we won it. I actually looked like I knew what I was doing out there, and the fans seemed to enjoy it. Well, I was feeling so confident after my first professional win that Buck O'Neil named Buck O'Neil as his starting pitcher the next day. Buck O'Neil the pitcher might still be out there if Buck O'Neil the manager hadn't taken him out after goodness knows how many runs and just a few innings. I think that was the only game the Monarchs ever lost in Wichita, by the way.

The last straw for the Monarchs came when the Philadelphia Athletics moved to Kansas City in '55. Tom Baird sold the franchise to Ted Rasberry, a Michigan-based entrepreneur who made the Monarchs a traveling team with headquarters in Grand Rapids. There were only four teams left in the Negro American League at the time, but Rasberry, to his credit, thought it was important to keep the flame alive. The Monarchs limped along until 1964, playing smaller and smaller towns, paying the players less and less money, abandoning the buses for station wagons. Occasionally, Satchel would show up to pitch for them, and every year they would make a trip to Kansas City. But interest in the Monarchs dwindled down to next-to-nothing, and they slipped quietly away without fanfare. The Indianapolis Clowns hung on for a while, but for the Negro leagues, the day-old bread was two days gone.

Yet when you look back, what people didn't realize, and still don't, was that we got the ball rolling on integration in our whole society. Remember, this was before Brown versus the Board of Education of Topeka. When Branch Rickey signed Jackie, Martin

Luther King was a student at Morris College. We showed the way it had to be done, by just keeping on and being the best we could. And the victory was finally complete when scouts began signing young black players in Alabama and Mississippi right out of high school. That was great, but it also meant these young blacks didn't need the Negro leagues anymore. That was the last nail in the coffin.

When I look at what happened after Jackie, I get a chill up my spine. But I also get a bittersweet feeling because I remember that a lot of people lost their whole way of life. That was another of those ironies, the hardest one. Not only did a black business die, other black businesses did, too, the ones that were dependent on black baseball and black entertainment. The Streets Hotel had to close because it couldn't compete with the Muehlebach Hotel downtown. The Vincennes in Chicago went out because the ballplayers and the entertainers were staying in the Loop now. Instead of the Woodside, they were staying in Times Square.

A way of life came to an end along with black baseball. But I guess it couldn't be any other way. The white-only hotels had to die, too, for integration to work, and that ended another way of life.

How do they say it in England? The king is dead,

long live the king? The Monarchs may have died, but they'll live on in our memories of the men who wore the uniform: Newt Allen, Bullet Joe Rogan, Turkey Stearnes, Ted Strong, Jackie Robinson, Ernie Banks, Elston Howard, Satchel Paige, and so many others. Even, I hope, Buck O'Neil.

Chapter 10

My Cub Scout Years

You may recall a story I told about my barn-storming days with the New York Tigers, and about how we had to sneak out of a rooming house in Shreveport, Louisiana, without paying the bill. I had sent the landlady a check for the full amount a few years later, but for some reason she had never cashed it.

Twenty-five years after we skipped, I was passing through Shreveport in my capacity as a scout for the Chicago Cubs. True to his word, Wid Matthews had offered me a full-time position with the Cubs when the Monarchs were sold, and it was my job to scour the country for the untapped talent in the predominantly black high schools and colleges which brought me to Shreveport one summer. Curiosity took me to that old rooming house. As I signed the register, I inquired about the landlady. The woman behind the desk said, "That was my mother. She passed away a few years ago." Then she looked at the book, and when she saw my name, she smiled and said, "I want to show you something."

She took me into the parlor, and there on the wall was my check, framed as if it were a diploma from a college. When it dawned on me that the landlady had hung it up there as a testament to faith restored, I was as proud of that check as I would have been of a degree from Howard—or Harvard—University. When I told her daughter the check was still good, she laughed and said, "It's much better where it is."

It's not always that easy to renew hope. I have known people who have never gotten past their bitterness and disappointment, and I wish I could have helped them with something as simple as a little piece of paper. Oh, sometimes I've steered a youngster toward baseball and away from a hard life, or talked a player out of quitting, or helped a guy get out of a slump. But what I've really tried to do is show them that the solution to their problem lies within. Have confidence. Tomorrow's another day. Count your blessings—they're *trouncing* your curses.

My blessings have been too numerous to count—loving parents, dedicated teachers, years spent in a baseball uniform (even if it was sometimes made of grass), a wonderful wife, loyal friends and teammates, a community like Kansas City. On top of all that, I was able to find another calling when my days as a Monarchs were over: scouting.

Here is what a scout lives for: I'm driving in my Plymouth Fury down a dirt road outside of Montgomery, Alabama. The road is so narrow that I'm thinking I must have taken the wrong fork a few miles back. Then, suddenly, I hear the crack of the bat and the noise of the crowd. Or is that my car backfiring and my engine whining? No, it's a ballgame, sure enough, because when I round the turn, there's a diamond cut out of the woods.

All around the field on this beautiful Saturday afternoon are people in lawn chairs, dipping into picnic baskets. They're there to watch two semipro teams. I had seen one of the teams a few weeks before, playing Tuskegee Institute. It was the Tuskegee team I was originally interested in, but the little centerfielder for the semipro team had caught my eye, and when I asked his manager where and when his next game was, he told me this field, on this Saturday afternoon.

Most of the players are in their late twenties and early thirties, much bigger and more polished than this teenager. But I like his swing, I like his arm, I like his quickness. Most of all, I like the fact that nobody else in pro baseball has ever seen this kid. Some of his teammates get big hits. One of them blasts a three-run homer into the woods. But they're not the ones I want. I feel a little like the prophet Samuel, checking out the sons of Jesse for a new king to anoint. The youngest son works the count to 3 and 2, waiting for the right pitch to hit, and when he gets it, he drives the ball deep to center, where the centerfielder catches it at the fence. He's the one, all right.

That's how I came to sign Oscar Gamble. He was the best prospect I had seen since Ernie Banks. Though Oscar didn't make the Hall of Fame, he did go on to a seventeen-year career in the majors, playing in two World Series for the New York Yankees.

If scouting were just a matter of signing the guys who hit the home runs and pitch the no-hitters, anybody could do it. But the major league prospect just might be the guy who has something special even though he struck out swinging or overthrew the third baseman from right field or walked nine batters. Tools we call them: speed, arm strength, range, hands, bat speed. Sometimes you can tell more about a player in one infield or batting practice than you can in nine innings. And give me the flamethrower with control problems over the offspeed pitcher with accuracy every time. You can teach certain aspects of the game. You can't just give a player ability.

I had a good eye for talent, and the Cubs respected that. But they didn't hire me just for my eye; they also hired me for my skin. That may make them seem prejudiced, but they were just being smart. The prejudiced teams were the ones who didn't have full-time black scouts, who made only halfhearted attempts to find black ballplayers—like the Red Sox did with Willie Mays.

As one of the only black scouts in baseball, I had a tremendous advantage. A white man watching a game between Savannah State and Morris Brown might as well hang a sign around his neck saying, "Major League Scout." Believe me, once the players knew there was a scout in the stands, they performed differently. On the other hand, I could sit in the stands and watch the players go about their natural business. Another edge I had was information; coaches and managers told me things they would never tell a white scout. And while the white scouts traveled in packs and shared their observations, I kept to myself, except for those nice times when Ora joined me after school was out.

I had one more ace up my sleeve. If a white scout

saw a black player he liked on a Saturday, he would go back to his hotel room, write a glowing report, then send it back to the home office. If I saw a kid I liked, I, too, would go back to my hotel and send off a glowing report. But on Sunday morning, I would be in church with his parents, and quite often I would sit down to Sunday supper with them, too. This was particularly important because one disadvantage I had was that I represented Chicago, the big, bad city up North. The families felt a little more comfortable sending their sons off with someone they had come to know and trust. And I took that responsibility very seriously.

Now, in those days, the Cubs were not a very good team. You might think that would also be a disadvantage in convincing players to sign with the Cubs instead of, say, the Yankees, but I would tell them, "With the Yankees, you'll be in the minor leagues for five years. With the Cubs, you've got a good chance to be in the majors in two or three years." That wasn't just a line; that was an unfortunate truth.

I first saw my second Hall-of-Famer playing for Southern University in Baton Rouge his freshman year. Lou Brock was a good example of a kid with tools and no polish. He must have hit .150 that first year at Southern, but I could see his speed and his power, and I knew it was only a matter of time before he blossomed. Sure enough, his sophomore year he batted .545, which was a conference record, with thirteen homers in twenty-seven games. Suddenly, scouts popped up like toadstools after a summer shower. When Southern beat a lot of predominantly white teams in a college tournament, Lou became a very hot property.

He cooled off some his junior year, but it was cold and rainy that spring, and while some scouts lost interest in him, I didn't. He was still undecided as to whether to finish school or turn pro. I encouraged him to get his degree, but I said that if he did decide to sign with a major league club, that was fine, too. Just give me the last shot. "Whatever they offer you," I told him, "I'll top it."

Sure enough, that summer I got a panicky call from someone in the Cubs' front office. "Buck, Lou Brock is in town trying out for the White Sox." I told him not to worry, I was on my way to Chicago. Well, the White Sox liked him so much they offered him fifteen thousand dollars, very good money at the time—we were signing players for around five thousand. But true to his word, Lou gave us the last shot, and after he worked out at Wrigley Field, we signed him right then and there for thirty thousand dollars.

Now, you Cub fans out there know the sad ending to the Lou Brock story. After two and a half very promising years with the Cubs, Lou was traded to the St. Louis Cardinals in the middle of the '64 season for pitcher Ernie Broglio. Not only did Lou help them into the World Series that year, he went on to set all-time stolen base records—season and career—and earn himself a plaque in Cooperstown. Ernie Broglio, meanwhile, came up with a sore arm and won seven games in his three seasons with the Cubs. People always ask me if I feel bad about the trade, but I just felt happy for Lou. In giving one of his sons the middle name of O'Neil, he gave me one of my greatest honors.

Lou also indirectly helped me out of a jam. After he had become an established star with the Cardinals, I was driving from Jackson, Mississippi, to Pineville, Louisiana, and because I was a little late for the game, my foot was a bit too heavy on the accelerator. A police car caught up to me, and when I pulled over, I was at first relieved to see that the officer was African-American. Maybe I wouldn't miss too much of the game after all. Smiling, I handed him my license and registration and said, "Hey, brother, how are you?" He just looked at my papers and said, "I'm not your brother." Uh-oh, I thought. I'm in trouble.

As he was getting out his book to write me a ticket, he looked again at my license and said, "John O'Neil. Do I know that name?"

"I'm Buck O'Neil, and I scout for the Chicago Cubs."

"Buck O'Neil, huh? Do you know Lou Brock?"

"Know Lou Brock? I *signed* Lou Brock."

Suddenly, the officer smiled. "Lou was a high school classmate of mine."

"How about *that*," I said. "You have any kids?"

"I've got a boy."

So I opened the trunk of my car and gave him a baseball, which he asked me to sign. Then he said, "You can go on now, but you better slow down. You were going pretty fast."

"I know," I told him. "I was going to Pineville to scout a game, and I was running late."

"Well," the officer said, "I'll escort you there," and he did. I got to the game without missing a pitch.

Piper Davis and I could have used that cop one night in Jackson, Mississippi. Piper, who used to manage against me when he ran the Birmingham Black Barons, was scouting for the Cardinals at the time, and we went to a Jackson State–Grambling game one afternoon with the idea that we would go to a high school game that night. But after the college game it started raining, so we decided to have dinner. After dinner it stopped raining, and I said, "Piper, we might as well go see that ballgame." Somebody at the hotel gave us directions, which we thought we were following. We didn't know exactly where we were going, but hey, there was the glare of the lights from the ballpark. Two white men were standing at the entrance to the parking lot, and I said to one of them, "This must be where the game is."

"Oh, yeah," said one of the guys. "This is where it is, all right."

We drove in and parked. Piper got out of the car and walked ahead while I fished around under the seat for my scouting book. Piper came back and said, "I don't know, Buck. This don't look right."

"What are you talking about?" I said. "Ain't nothin' but a ballgame."

Piper didn't say anything, I found my book, got out of the car, and headed toward the park. Our view to the field was blocked by the stadium entrance, but when we got within sight of the field, I saw what Piper was talking about. In front of the pitcher's mound was a flatbed truck. And on that truck was a man in full Ku Klux Klan regalia—the "pitcher" was a grand dragon of the KKK. Everyone around him, and everyone in the stands, had on a white hood and robe. Over by first base was a barbecue pit with a pig roasting on a spit. With the smoke hanging over the field, I thought we had wandered into hell, and indeed, we had. "No, Piper," I said. "This ain't no ballgame."

We got back to the car as fast as we could without

drawing attention to ourselves, and we sprayed gravel as we sped out of that parking lot. The two men at the gate were laughing so hard they were in tears, doubled over and gasping for breath. I'm sure they told that story for years. I know Piper and I did.

As time passed, my duties with the Cubs expanded beyond scouting. I got a call from the front office one year to go see our Class C club in St. Cloud, Minnesota. It seemed that Lou Brock and some of the other black players on the team were grumbling about the way the manager was treating them, in contrast to the way he was treating the white players. The manager, a guy from the South, acted like a father to the whites and a boss to the blacks. The fact that Lou had three years of college and this man had only a high school education didn't help matters.

I sat down with the manager and explained that if he was going to be a father figure, fine, just be one to all the players. If he wanted to act like a boss, well, then he better boss around the white guys, too. When he started to roll his eyes, I tried another tactic. "Every team in our organization has at least one black player," I pointed out. "If you want to manage in the Cubs system, you're going to have to get used to it." That argument he understood. And don't you know, he became one of the organization's best handlers of young talent, black or white.

Another time, I do believe it was 1959, I got another emergency call, this one from John Holland, who was the general manager. I was in Baton Rouge, scouting Southern University, when Holland told me, "Billy's gone home."

"What?" I knew he was talking about Billy Williams, but I couldn't believe it. He was our best prospect, and he was in San Antonio tearing up the Class AA pitching in the Texas League.

"Billy's gone back to Mobile," said Holland. "Go down there and find out what the hell is wrong with him."

"I'm on my way," I said.

Billy Williams was the last player I expected to jump a team. He was already in his fourth professional season, he never demonstrated any emotional problems, and like I said, he was having an outstanding season. As it turned out, he had gotten a phone call from his older brother, Frank, who told him how great the weather was in Mobile, and how good the fishing and the swimming were, and because Billy was very much a small-town, family kid, the phone call made him homesick. He got a teammate to drive him to the railroad station where he caught a train back to Alabama.

And that's where I came in. I hadn't signed Billy, but I had gotten to know him and his family pretty well during his first year of pro ball in Class D. So when I showed up at his parents' home, I was as friendly as could be. I shook hands all around, making out like it was just a social call. I said nothing about Billy jumping the team. We chatted for a while, and then I took them all out to dinner.

The next night his mother fixed dinner, and after the table was cleared, I said to Billy, "C'mon. Let's go out to the ballyard. There's a player I want to see." This was just a pretense, of course, although you never knew what you might find in Mobile, the garden of such delights as Henry Aaron and Willie McCovey. When we got to the ballpark—it was just a little sand-lot league—Billy was mobbed by the younger ball-players. "Billy, we hear you're doin' great." "Billy, have you met Ernie Banks?" "Billy, what brings you home?"

They treated him like a superstar, and I could see that Billy enjoyed the attention. I spent five days in Mobile with the Williams family, and I never said one thing to him about going back to San Antonio. I never had to. What sold him was those other hungry young ballplayers. He saw what a great thing he had going, and he knew that if he blew it, there were a hundred guys waiting in line to take his place.

Out of the blue one day, Billy said, "I think I'm ready to go back." I called the office to give John Holland the news, and he said, "Put him on a bus and send him back to Texas." I said, "I'm not putting him on any bus. I'm putting him in my car and driving him to San Antonio." On our way to Texas we talked about a lot of things. It seems that in addition to being homesick, he was having a little crisis of confidence. I told him one day he was going to be right up there with Ernie Banks and the other big stars. "Do you really think so?" he said. "I know so," I said. Sure enough, Billy Williams is right up there with Ernie Banks—in Cooperstown.

By 1962 I was a sort of unofficial coach for the Cubs, working with the players during spring training in Mesa, Arizona, and even after the season started in Chicago. When other teams complained about my presence in the dugout, the umpires made me leave. The Cubs solved the problem in June of '62 by making me an official coach. I didn't think it was that big a deal at the time, but suddenly I was in *Sports Illustrated* and *Ebony* and all the papers. At the age of fifty, I became the first Negro to coach in the major leagues.

The clippings seem a trifle dated now. In the *Ebony* profile, there's a picture of me sitting between Billy and George, and the caption reads: "Gabbing with Billy Williams and George Altman, O'Neil shares their problems. A bridge and golf enthusiast, he attributes his superb physical condition to good dieting, espe-

212

cially enjoys a plate of beans, corn bread and a side dish of greens."

In 1962 the Cubs were in their second year of Phil Wrigley's infamous College of Coaches: Four coaches were rotated on a month-to-month basis as the "head coach," because Mr. Wrigley felt the pressure of being a manager for a year was too much for any one man. It was a ridiculous idea, although I was quoted in the *Ebony* article as saying it was a "wonderful innovation" that would "be adopted by most teams." What was I supposed to say?

Anyway, when John Holland named me a coach, he vaguely left open the possibility that I would one day become part of the rotation. I soon found out there was no chance of that happening. We were playing the Houston Colt .45s, and Charlie Metro, our manager of the moment, was thrown out of the game. So Elvin Tappe, the third base coach, took over, and Lou Klein moved over to third. Lo and behold, Tappe gets thrown out, which means Klein is now at the helm. Who's on third?

I would have been the natural choice, and I could sense the buzzing up and down the bench. But the call came down from upstairs, and Fred Martin, the pitching coach, trotted in from the bullpen to stand in the third base box. Nothing against Fred Martin, but I was far more qualified to coach third base than he. After

forty years in baseball and ten years as a manager, I
was pretty sure I knew when to wave somebody home
and when to make him put on the brakes. I would
have gotten a huge thrill out of being on a major league
field during the game. Not going out there that day
was one of the few disappointments I've had in over
sixty years in baseball.

Afterwards, I found out from Charlie Metro that it
was Charlie Grimm who made the call. Metro and I
were scouting the same game years later when he told
me, "Grimm told us, 'Whatever you do, don't ever let
Buck coach on that line. Especially third base. If he
does, somebody's going to lose their job because he's
going to take it.' "

Grimm was the guy they called Jolly Cholly, and in
his playing days he was an outstanding first baseman,
a good hitter without the great power. He was sort of
the Buck O'Neil of the major leagues. Anyway, he was
a favorite of Mr. Wrigley, and over the years he held a
variety of positions with the club: manager, broad-
caster, executive. But I was not a favorite of Grimm's
because every spring, when I managed against him in
intersquad games, I would beat him. The reason was
simple: He chose the white players and let me have
the black players. If he had had Lou Brock, George
Altman, Billy Williams, and Ernie Banks, he might
have won.

Lou and Billy still kid me about the expressions I used on the bench with the Cubs. "If the sucker wants to help you . . ." Lou will say when we all get together, "let the sucker help you," Billy will finish. That's what I always said when a batter swung at a ball way outside the strike zone. "Suck it up!" I would shout at an infielder charging a ground ball. "Come on up here and get your killing!" I'd holler before a guy stepped in against me in batting practice.

I wanted to do more than just cheerlead, of course. I was flattered after the season when Doc Young of the *Chicago Defender* championed me as the next Cubs manager, but it was wishful thinking on his part and no more than a pipedream for me. The Cubs named Bob Kennedy their full-time manager for the 1963 season. That was also the year the Pirates made my old protégé Gene Baker the first black manager of a minor league team, Batavia in the lowly New York–Penn League.

Normally, it takes a player four to six years to move up from the New York–Penn League to the majors. But it took baseball another twelve years to finally elevate a black man to the post of major league manager. That happened in 1975, when the Cleveland Indians made Frank Robinson their player-manager. Progress in organized baseball was painfully slow; still is. There are far too few black scouts, executives, coaches, and managers. The proportion of blacks to whites in the front office is nowhere near what it is on the field.

And it's not just the numbers; it's the language. I still hear African-American players referred to as "articulate," as if we should be surprised a black man speaks so well. I still see a black player labeled as an underachiever, while a white player who carries the same stats is called an overachiever. Joe DiMaggio? Why, when people talk of him, they talk of his grace and his intelligence and his consistency. Willie Mays? He was "naturally gifted," as if he didn't have to work as hard as DiMaggio to become a great ballplayer. Poppycock. From 1949 to 1962, eleven of the fourteen National League MVP trophies went to black men, and all of them, including Mays, Aaron, and Banks, worked damn hard to get those trophies.

In 1964 I returned to scouting full time. In truth, it was what I most enjoyed. I loved the thrill of the hunt, the give-and-take with high school and college coaches, the chance to track down some of my old friends from the Negro leagues. Plus, when the Cubs needed me for something more, I was always around. One winter, I sat with Ernie Banks looking at some videotapes, found a flaw in his swing, and resurrected his career. Another time, the Cubs had acquired a pitcher from the Phillies with the intention of making him a reliever. I suggested they make Ferguson Jenkins a starter.

Scouting had evolved quite a bit over the years. The onset of the amateur draft meant a club could acquire a player who had never sat down to Sunday dinner with one of its scouts. It meant that a scout could no longer hide a player—the road to Oscar Gamble had been paved over.

There were other changes, too. College football and basketball coaches were stealing away some of our best prospects. Agents were dictating terms to us instead of parents. But you had to go with the flow, and I learned to adjust. In 1975 I recommended three picks to the Cubs: a big kid from the little town of Castor, Louisiana, named Lee Smith; another high school pitcher out of Baton Rouge named Michael Taylor; and a fine young outfielder from Florida A&M named Andre Dawson. Unfortunately, I ranked them in just that order. The scouting department was able to land my first two picks, so we got the two pitchers, and we let the Montreal Expos get Dawson.

In 1981 I was high on a right-handed power hitter for Wichita State, name of Joe Carter. So were a lot of other scouts. We had the second pick, and we took him, but Joe also had the option of not accepting our offer and returning to Wichita State his senior year. Complicating matters, Joe's advisor was his coach,

Gene Stephenson, who wouldn't have minded having him back for another year. I had to find some way of making everybody happy. So what I did was promise Joe and Gene that he would get more money than the first draft pick in the country, a pitcher from Oral Roberts named Mike Moore. That had real appeal to Gene, who could tell his recruits that Joe Carter got more money than anyone in the draft. It was just a little more, maybe a thousand dollars, but it worked. "Now you're on my street!" Gene told me when he saw our offer.

As with Lou Brock, the Cubs traded away Carter before he became a star. But as with Brock, I have followed Joe's career with pride and joy. I could not have been happier when he hit that home run to win the 1993 World Series. As you know, it gave the Toronto Blue Jays their second consecutive world championship. As I well know, it gave a second consecutive World Series trophy to Cito Gaston, their African-American manager.

Chapter 11

Love What You Do

Satchel used to say, "The past is a long and twisty road." Well, his road was longer and twistier than most. He did a lot of barnstorming, of course, and at one point he was the guest celebrity of the Harlem Globetrotters. He went out to Hollywood to make a movie, *The Wonderful Country,* in which he played a cavalry sergeant. He once announced he was going to run for a seat in the Missouri legislature, but that went against rule number five of Satchel's six rules on how to stay young, which was, "Avoid running at all times," so nothing much came of his candidacy.

Funny thing about those rules, which you have

probably heard at one time or another. They first appeared in a *Collier's* magazine article about Satchel, and they were the creation of the writer, Richard Donovan, who was trying to find a way to use some lively quotes left over in his notebook. Just to get them out of the way, here they are:

How to Stay Young

1. Avoid fried meats which angry up the blood.
2. If your stomach disputes you, lie down and pacify it with cool thoughts.
3. Keep the juices flowing by jangling around gently as you move.
4. Go very light on the vices, such as carrying on in society. The social ramble ain't restful.
5. Avoid running at all times.
6. Don't look back. Something might be gaining on you.

That last rule landed Satchel in *Bartlett's Familiar Quotations* on the same page as Adlai Stevenson. The rules became so much a part of his identity that he had them printed up on the business cards he used to hand out. He once recited them at a seminar on aging given by the American College of Physicians.

On the ballfield, Satchel got one more chance to show how young he could stay. In 1965, Charles O. Finley, the owner of the Kansas City Athletics, signed this fifty-nine-year-old man as a pitcher. It was pretty much a publicity stunt, on the order of that Charley O. mule that Finley kept around the ballpark. Finley set Satchel up in the bullpen in a rocking chair, with a nurse rubbing liniment on his arm—the way Jewbaby Floyd used to do. As you can imagine, the other Athletics weren't too happy about this old man taking away some of their limelight, especially since he never pitched in a game. But Satchel had a surprise for them.

Finley instructed his manager, Haywood Sullivan, to start Satchel on September 25 in Kansas City against the Boston Red Sox. Well, old Satch pitched three shutout innings, giving up only one hit, and that was to Carl Yastrzemski, who wound up in the Hall of Fame. They let him throw some warmup pitches in the fourth so Sullivan could take him out to a standing ovation, after which the fans lit matches and sang silly songs like, "The Old Gray Mare" and "Old Rocking Chair." After the game, Satchel told the press, "Everybody doubted me on the ballclub. They'll have more confidence in me. Now I'll stay in shape because they know what I can do."

But Finley was only after the publicity, and it was cruel of him to let Satchel think he was going to pitch again. He never did. But that one appearance did get my friend in the record book as the oldest player ever to appear in a major league game. In 1967, Satchel came out with his autobiography, *Maybe I'll Pitch Forever*, a book I highly recommend if you can find it.

The Atlanta Braves signed Satchel a few years later to be a coach and batting practice pitcher and to give him the necessary service time for his major league pension. It was a very nice thing for them to do because, quite frankly, Satchel could always use the money. After all, he had seven children, the youngest of whom was born when he was fifty-seven. People still ask me if Lahoma, who bore all those children, ever found out why he called me Nancy. Of course she did. She *knew* Satchel. She loved the story. I never would have told it if she hadn't heard it from him first.

In 1971, Satchel—and the rest of us Negro league players—got the recognition that was so long overdue when he was inducted into the Hall of Fame. He came in the front door, but the original plan was for him to go in the back door: into a special wing for Negro-leaguers. A lot of people, black and white, were angry when that plan was announced, and I think Satchel shook them up when he said, "The only change is that baseball has turned Paige from a second-class citizen into a second-class immortal." The outcry was such that Commissioner Bowie Kuhn reversed the decision and put Satchel in the same room with Ruth and Mathewson and Jackie Robinson. "I am the proudest man on the face of the earth today," Satchel told the folks in Cooperstown. Then he turned to Bill Veeck, who had drawn a lot of criticism for signing the forty-two-year-old Satchel for the Indians back in '48. "And I finally got you off the hook."

In 1981 they made a fine, made-for-television movie about Mr. Paige entitled *Don't Look Back* and starring Louis Gossett, Jr., as Satch. Besides being a wonderful actor, Gossett looks an awful lot like Satchel. They mixed up some facts, and they oversimplified the rivalry between barnstorming black and white all-star teams, but they got Satchel right, in all his greatness, his humor, his intelligence, his sensitivity. He was truly a remarkable man, and one of the very great blessings of my life was having known him as a friend.

In 1982 we got the parks and recreation commissioners in Kansas City to buy a weed-covered ballyard called O'Hara Field and modernize and upgrade and call it Leroy Satchel Paige Stadium. Satch was ailing at the time, dying of heart trouble and emphysema, and he was in a wheelchair, hooked up to some oxygen, when we dedicated the field on June 5. A lot of the old Monarchs were there: Hilton Smith, Jesse Williams, Willard Brown, Earl Taborn, Chico Renfroe, Quincy Trouppe. Satchel seemed to be really touched by all the attention and love that day, and I believed him when he said, "This is the happiest day of my life. Nobody on earth could feel as good as I do now."

Three days later, I got the phone call. Satchel had died peacefully. He was seventy-five at the end of his long and twisty road. His death made the evening news shows and the front pages of all the newspapers. But of all the things I read and heard, I particularly liked what one woman newscaster had to say. "Satchel Paige died yesterday," she said, "but, oh, how he lived!" Even though she didn't know the half of it, I couldn't have said it better myself.

I did get to say a few words at his funeral in Forest Hill Cemetery on June 12. While I don't precisely re-call my eulogy, I do remember saying, "People say it's a shame that Satchel Paige never got to pitch against the best. But who's to say he didn't?"

By chance, the Seattle Mariners were in town then to play the Royals, and Rene Lachemann, the manager of the Mariners, took the time to attend the funeral. Not many people know this, but Rene was a nineteen-year-old catcher with the A's when Satchel pitched for the club in '65, and he caught him a lot on the sidelines and in batting practice. Rene said that even then, Satchel had tremendous control, a fastball as good as some guys in the majors, and more than enough stuff to get a lot of guys out. That was nice to hear.

Even in death, Satchel was on the move. A few years after his burial, the folks at Forest Hill agreed to transfer his remains to a more accessible and obvious plot. If you're ever in Kansas City, you might want to stop by Forest Hill Cemetery and visit with Satchel. He and Lahoma, who passed away in 1986, share a gravesite on an island of green in the middle of the cemetery's main road. We're quite proud of the tombstones we put there in 1989, pictures etched in stone of Satchel and Lahoma. The inscription on Satchel's memorial tells of how he got his nickname, ending with the line, "And so Leroy became Satchel, and Satchel became legend." And under that are written the six rules on how to stay young.

I see great wisdom in those words of advice. But if Satchel will permit me, I would like to add a seventh rule. And that is this:

7. Love what you do.

Uh-huh. Simple as that. Love what you do in life, whether that be shoemaking, lawyering, writing, waiting tables, selling, doctoring, dishwashing, teaching, playing ball, mothering, fathering, policing, engineering, truckdriving, searching for the cure to cancer, firefighting, scouting, tailoring, filmmaking, etcetera, etcetera. Doesn't matter how much money you make. Doesn't matter the per capita income of your neighborhood. I have known bellhops who were happier and a lot better off than chairmen of the board. Love what you do. Take pride in it, take joy in it, and you'll live longer. And if you don't love it, if your job is making you unhappy, if you're on welfare—a terrible innovation that only robs people of their self-esteem—then find something to do that you *will* love.

I never stopped loving baseball, and I've been in it now for over sixty years. Sometimes it seems kind of frivolous to devote so much time to what is essentially a kid's game, but I know what joy it has brought me, what joy it has brought others. I like to think that if I hadn't found baseball, I might have found teaching. *That* I think is the most noble profession, to pass on to younger people not only knowledge and information but also hopes and dreams. I watched Ora do it for more than forty years—heavens, she's still teaching me things—and I saw how she spread her love of teaching to generations of students.

I just happened to luck into baseball. Since I was a pup, I've been following that bouncing ball in one way or another. I played with Satchel Paige, I managed Ernie Banks, I coached Lou Brock, I scouted Lee Smith. I've said it before, I'll say it now, and I'll say it again: I was right on time.

Back in 1988, I figured my time was up, so I retired after thirty-two years with the Cubs to spend more time with Ora, who had just retired from teaching, and to see if I could get my golf score for eighteen holes down to my age, which was seventy-seven at the time. (I have reached that goal, which is actually a lot easier these days.)

But right after I announced my retirement, John Schuerholz, the general manager of the Royals, called. He offered me a job as a special assignment scout for the team. Working for Kansas City meant considerably less travel, which was good, and that I could watch games from those great scout seats behind home plate, which was even better. Watching baseball games had become so much a part of the rhythm of my life that I had begun to wonder what I was going to do with those free evenings.

The job with the Royals turned out to be even more rewarding than I expected. George Brett says I'm the team's insurance against a long losing streak. I love stopping by the clubhouse before a game to cheer up a fella in a slump, to tell the younger players about the Negro leagues, to show them what shadow ball really looked like. Up in the stands, I love those few minutes before a game, when the ushers and fans and other scouts stop by to pay a call. And when the game starts, I love watching those great athletes play ball.

I am not one of those crabby old-timers who thinks that the players of today couldn't hold a candle to the players of his era. No, they're probably faster and stronger and quicker than we were. I just wonder if they have as good a time as we did. The one player I see now whom I would've loved to have played with is Ken Griffey, Jr. There are dozens of other great players: Frank Thomas, Cal Ripken, Tony Gwynn, Greg Maddux, Joe Carter. But Griffey stands out because not only does he have a world of talent, he also plays the game with real joy. He loves what he does.

So, Satchel, forgive me for adding that last rule. Besides, I don't think "How to Stay Young" was the best thing you ever said (or somebody said you said) anyway. No, my favorite Satchel Paige quote is this:

"Never let your head hang down. Never give up and sit down and grieve. Find another way. And don't pray when it rains if you don't pray when the sun shines."

Chapter 12

Got to Give It Up

I have hit home runs against the best pitchers. I have hit grand slam homers. I have stolen home. I have hit for the cycle. I have met President Truman. I have met President Clinton. I even hugged Hillary. But the greatest thrill of my life was receiving my high school diploma—at the age of eighty-three.

I know—I'm a little old for the senior prom. Senior *citizen* prom would be more like it. But there's a story behind this brand-new diploma for this old relic, and it starts with the Ken Burns film. I guess when I started talking in *Baseball* about the celery fields in Sarasota, some folks in Sarasota were listening, and they de-

cided to name a ballpark after me, the Twin Lakes
Park where the Baltimore Orioles train each spring
and where the Royals used to have their baseball acad-
emy. I was naturally quite honored, but I was also
tickled because now both Satchel and I would have
our own ballfields. He might have called mine Nancy
Park.

About seventy years ago, I watched Sarasota High
School being built. It was a place I could walk by, a
place I wanted desperately to go to, but a place I could
not enter. When I finished elementary school in 1926,
my grandmother sat me down and said, "John, you
can't go to Sarasota High School. Sarasota High School
is not for black kids." I shed a few tears at the time,
but she said, "Don't cry. One day all kids will go to
Sarasota High School."

Well, I guess they heard about that, too, in Sarasota,
and they decided to correct the injustice when I went
home in the spring of 1995 for the dedication of the
ballfield. Actually, I go to Sarasota nearly every spring
to visit my relatives, but this time the Buck O'Neil
Reception Committee rolled out the red carpet. On
Tuesday I spoke to classes at the Emma Booker Elementary School, the Emma Booker Middle School,
and the Emma Booker High School—that should tell
you just how wonderful a woman Mrs. Booker was.
On Wednesday they dedicated the baseball complex

after me. Frank Robinson, the first black manager, was there, and so was Ken Burns. I met with some of the Orioles' minor leaguers. I told them that if they wanted it bad enough, to go after it. I told them, and I'm telling you, don't let anyone put a needle in your arm, don't let anyone put something up your nose that doesn't belong there. Your body is God's temple. I'm proud to say that I was six-foot-two and 190 pounds when I played, and I'm six-foot-two and 190 pounds now. I still have my five senses. I still have all my organs. *And some of them work.*

Actually, I gave a lot of speeches and talks that week, and I'm afraid I tend to repeat myself a bit. But one thing I always repeat—on purpose—is this: "Give it up." You got to give it up. You got to give people love. I can honestly say I love everybody and I hate no one. I hate cancer, which has touched so many of our lives, and I hate AIDS, and I hate hatred—men remain in ignorance so long as they hate. But I hate no human being.

Sometimes at the end of my speeches I ask the audience to join hands and sing a little song. It goes like this: "The greatest thing in all my life is loving you." At first, the audience is a little shy about holding hands and singing that corny song, but by and by, they all clasp one another's hands and the voices get louder and louder. They give it up. Got to give it up.

A lot of my old colleagues from the Negro leagues were in Sarasota for Buck O'Neil Week—I got a ballpark *and* a week named after me. I saw Harold Hair, John Kennedy, Curly Williams. Eugene White, and from that old Sarasota Tigers team, Carlos Suarez. A lot of old friends. But I also made sure to visit my parents and my sister Fanny in the family cemetery plot over by Highway 301.

That was on a Thursday. On Friday I went to Sarasota High School to receive my diploma. I didn't know quite what to expect, but I certainly didn't expect two thousand people to show up to watch one old man get his sheepskin. I didn't expect all the cheerleaders and dancers and flag girls and chorus members. I didn't expect the cake and the fireworks and varsity baseball jersey and all the nice things people gave me and said about me. Dr. Foster read a lovely poem about an old man who swims across a wide chasm, only to start building a bridge back to the other side so that men younger than him will have an easier time crossing. At one point, when there was a slight lull, I heard a young voice ring out, "We love you, Buck." Got to give it up.

Sixty-nine years after I cried because I couldn't go to Sarasota High School, I was crying because I was about to graduate. I was almost too choked up to speak. But I did. I told those students that I had talked to my parents and my sister the day before. And in my conversation, I let Mama and Papa and Fanny know that I would be going to Sarasota High School the next day to graduate. You can't see them, I told the students, but they're here today. I feel them.

The diploma they gave me is now one of my most prized possessions. I like what the principal, Dan Kennedy, said when he gave it to me. "I certify," he said, "that John Jordan Buck O'Neil has met *and exceeded* the requirements for graduation from Sarasota High School." It seems I picked up some extra credits along my own long and twisty road.

As good as I felt that day, I felt bad, too. Somewhere deep down, it still hurts to know that for one black boy from Sarasota it took almost seventy years to get that diploma. And it hurts just as bad to know that for other black boys, who have opportunities I never did, seventy years still won't be enough.

But I figure I can play in that game, too. Not long ago, I was invited by Miss Inge Hanson of Harlem RBI—which stands for Reviving Baseball in Inner Cities—to come back to Harlem, this time as an "elder statesman," not a wide-eyed kid in a country suit, to hand out achievement awards to kids from the streets of Harlem who made it good through this fine program.

Now, I go to a lot of awards dinners, but this was

different because I was surrounded by kids who never heard of me. But it was one of the biggest kicks in my life to see that a mix of baseball and education—the same mix that did me so much good—can still work.

Actually, RBI was started in Los Angeles in 1989 by a Florida Marlins scout named John Young, who wanted to use baseball as a tool to get kids away from gangs and drugs and crime. He got major league baseball to get it going with a grant, and then local businesses came in. Since then, about 1,200 kids from eight to eighteen have played in the RBI league out there, which has something like forty teams. Today RBI programs, underwritten by major league baseball and local sponsors, are going strong in Kansas City and St. Louis, and of course in Harlem.

The main thing about these programs is that they've rescued baseball from the dead along with the kids. Truth is, black kids had stopped playing baseball and baseball had stopped selling itself to the inner city; they just sold it to the suburbs. The black kids were just playing basketball and football. This is why RBI is trying to rejuvenate baseball in the inner city. And we want these kids to play baseball. Right now the majority of blacks in the majors are from Latin countries. There are a lot of kids in our cities who are good athletes, but they'll never play pro basketball or pro football because you have to be big and quick to play those sports. But in baseball you can be five-foot-nine and be a superstar. It's the ordinary man's game.

I want to see as much enthusiasm for baseball in the inner city as there is for basketball. Kids now shoot hoops all night long under the lights in the playgrounds. I want them to do that with baseball, and if they do, they'll be bringing other kids with them because they'll need someone to throw the ball back to them.

So that's the baseball part of the program. The other part is all about education. RBI has afterschool tutoring and guidance counselors. And there's a learning center right next to the ballfield, at 102nd Street and First Avenue. And guess what? It works! These kids are staying in school. That's a tough neighborhood, man. It's so easy to go bad. When I met some of them, I praised God they were able to go the right way. One kid, Manny Agosto, is eighteen. He's the father of a little baby. His mother has cancer. He can talk all day about guns going off in his neighborhood. But Manny didn't give in to the pressures. He graduated from high school, went to St. John's University, and got a 3.0 grade-point average. Without RBI, without baseball, it might have been a whole different story, maybe a tragic story.

I get letters from kids like Manny all the time, and every one is a revelation. Their lives have been changed, and they're grateful to me for taking an interest in them. But, really, it's baseball they're thanking. Baseball is what gave them a bunch of self-esteem, just like it did me.

And you know what? These kids didn't know me before their elders told them who I was. But I was amazed that they knew not only who Jackie Robinson was, but also Satchel Paige and Josh Gibson! These are hip city kids, so that must mean the word has survived. And now they know me. At first, they might not have believed that this eighty-four-year-old guy had been a pretty fair ballplayer. But when I did the limbo at their banquet and went under that bar like a kid, they knew this old man had some athletic talent in him!

I remember what I told those kids that day, and I meant it. I told them about some of the things I got to do on a baseball field, things I really enjoyed doing. "But," I said, "right now, I'd rather be here with you than any place I've ever been."

Yes, I've been to a lot of places. I have a few years left in me, but I know my road will be coming to an end soon. In the meantime, I still have the Negro Leagues Museum business to keep me busy, and I hope you'll come visit us the next time you're in Kansas City. It's worth a visit to Kansas City just for the museum, and in a few years, when we're joined up with the Jazz Museum, 18th and Vine will be hopping again. I will remain active as long as I can on the Veterans Committee. And because the Lord has kept me on this earth to bear witness to the days and glories and men (and women) of the Negro leagues, I will continue to give speeches, knowing that my father is sitting on the side on some of those celery crates, listening.

Some of those speeches will be about not only paying tribute to the Negro-leaguers but remembering them in a personal way—with some kind of financial help. There's an organization I'd like to plug called BAT, the Baseball Alumni Team, which is run by Joe Garagiola and Joe Black—a great pitcher for the Dodgers who got his start in the Negro leagues. They're helping destitute Negro league ballplayers. There are a lot of guys like that. We recently celebrated the seventy-fifth anniversary of the Negro leagues here in Kansas City, and some of the guys were blind, some were in wheelchairs. It'd be nice for them to live out their lives a little easier.

Major league baseball is starting to help guys like that out, but I'm not going to say it's about time because, truthfully, they don't owe us anything. They don't have to make good on old sins, because our own owners could have found a way to provide for us and they didn't. Heck, the majors didn't do that with their own players for a long time. Whatever baseball does for us, I'm thankful for it. But if baseball—and I mean the players and the owners both—should give some kind of pension to these men, it would be a huge lift.

I'm pleased to say that modern-day athletes are starting to appreciate the Negro league ballplayers. Not long ago it wasn't like that. Ours was a period of history that a lot of people wanted to forget. The feeling was, "Man, don't bring that up to me." And that was on both sides of the fence, black and white. A lot of people want to forget those days as if they never happened.

But now a lot of players empathize more with the Negro leagues than even a Willie Mays or a Henry Aaron did. These young kids are coming to the museum all the time, asking lots of questions. Some players like Delino DeShields wear their socks high to honor *our* style. So maybe there's been a rebirth of interest.

For black players especially, that's important. A lot of black players don't realize what they owe to us. They never knew the kind of segregation we faced, but if they could turn their thoughts away from the money they make, they might identify with us old-timers, because apart from the salaries, they still face the problem of racism in our society. I don't see too many black athletes getting endorsements here in

Kansas City. Things change, but they haven't changed enough.

The thing is, white kids even today know about Ty Cobb and Babe Ruth. Black kids should know about Cool Papa Bell and Turkey Stearnes. African-American heroes didn't start with Willie Mays. This is their history, and I hope I've helped to give it life.

The newfound popularity of the Negro leagues has come along a little too late to save the Monarchs, but it's gratifying nonetheless. It's wonderful that folks are remembering the people who built the bridge across the chasm of prejudice, not just the men who later crossed it.

Well, I think it's about time to close the book on this book before I start boring you. Besides, I've got a game to go to. I just might see for the first time the next Josh Gibson or Satchel Paige.

Just remember: The greatest thing in all my life is loving you. Sing it. Together.

Index

Index

Index

Index